Capability-Based Computer Systems

Capability-Based
Computer Systems

Henry M. Levy

DIGITAL PRESS

Printed in the United States of America

10 9 8 7 6 5 4 3 2 1

Documentation Number: EY-00025-DP
ISBN: 0-932376-22-3

Library of Congress Cataloging in Publication Data

Levy, Henry M., 1952–
  Capability-based computer systems.

  Bibliography: p. 205
  Includes index.
  1. Computer architecture. 2. Operating systems (Computers) 3. System design. I. Title.
  QA76.9.A73L48 1983   621.3819′58   83-21029
  ISBN 0-932376-22-3

Trademarks

Bell Laboratories: UNIX. Burroughs Corporation: B5000. Cambridge University: CAP. Control Data Corporation: CDC 6400, SCOPE. Digital Equipment Corporation: DEC, LSI-11, PDP-1, PDP-11, TOPS-20. Hewlett-Packard Company: HP 3000. Intel Corporation: iAPX 432, iMAX, Intel 8086. IBM: CPF, IBM 370, IBM System/38, SWARD. International Computers Ltd.: Basic Language Machine. Plessey Telecommunications Ltd. Plessey System 250. Xerox Corporation: Smalltalk.

iv

In Memory of **Manny** *and* **Sonia**

Preface

The purpose of this book is to provide a single source of information about capability-based computer systems. Although capability systems have existed for nearly two decades, only recently have they appeared in architecture and operating system textbooks. Much has been written about capability systems in the technical literature, but finding this information is often difficult.

This book is an introduction, a survey, a history, and an evaluation of capability- and object-based computer systems. It is intended for students, computer professionals, and computer-system designers. The book assumes a knowledge of the assembly-level architecture of at least one computer, an understanding of memory addressing and virtual memory systems, and some familiarity with operating systems. It can be used as a tutorial or reference text in advanced undergraduate or graduate courses in computer organization, computer architecture, or operating systems.

Chapter 1 introduces the concept of a capability and examines the use of capabilities in computer systems. It compares and contrasts simplified models of capability and conventional addressing and protection systems. The object-based design methodology is introduced, and the use of capabilities to support object-based systems is discussed.

Chapter 2 describes machines that preceded the formal definition of capabilities but had similar addressing mechanisms. Developed in the late 1950s and early 1960s, these machines include the Burroughs B5000, the Rice University computer, and the Basic Language Machine. Chapter 3 examines the Dennis and Van Horn hypothetical supervisor that introduced the concept of capability, and the early university attempts to implement that concept: the MIT PDP-1 system, the Chicago Magic Number Machine, and the CAL-TSS system.

Chapter 4 describes the Plessey System 250. Built in the U.K., the Plessey 250 multiprocessor was the first commercially available capability-based computer system. Also built in the U.K., Cambridge University's CAP computer system, examined in Chapter 5, was the first successful university implementation of capability hardware.

Chapters 6 and 7 concentrate on two capability-based multiprocessor operating systems built at Carnegie-Mellon University: Hydra and STaROS. These systems were the first major object-based systems and used capabilities to provide object-level addressing and protection.

Chapters 8 and 9 examine the new generation of capability/object-based systems designed for the commercial marketplace: the IBM System/38 and the Intel iAPX 432. The System/38 is the first use of object-based methodology to build a business-oriented computer system. The Intel 432 is the first highly-integrated object-based microprocessor. Both systems use object-based methodology to raise the level of the architecture interface. This allows them to support sophisticated operating-systems operations in hardware.

Chapter 10 reviews many of the important design issues in capability- and object-based systems in light of the implementations discussed throughout the book. Alternative implementation decisions and their implications are examined.

Each survey section presents the important features of a particular system. For this reason, different systems may be described at somewhat different levels. However, all systems are discussed in sufficient detail to give the reader an understanding of both the concepts and the low-level capability addressing and object-support mechanisms. An important goal of the book is examination of hardware and operating-system implementations of capabilities. Although all of the systems begin with a similar conceptual view of capabilities, the implementations are vastly different.

All attempts have been made to see that the system presentations are accurate, and most of the sections have been reviewed by one or more of the system's designers. Still, these discussions should not be taken as the final word and the interested reader is referred to the latest technical literature for more detailed study. Each section contains suggestions for further reading, and a complete bibliography on capability and object systems is included at the end of the book.

Acknowledgments

I was fortunate to have as reviewers many of the creative people who helped design and build the systems described in the book. I would like to thank them for providing an interesting topic of study and for lending their valuable time. I was privileged to have the benefit of the technical and historical insight of Maurice Wilkes and Earl Van Horn. Pete Lee and Guy Almes provided detailed reviews (and re-reviews) of the entire manuscript. These contributed heavily to the book. I would like to thank the many other people who provided critiques of individual chapters.

This book is the result of a study that began when I was a Digital Equipment Corporation resident at the University of Washington. I would like to thank Bill Strecker for supporting my stay at Washington and for providing a creative working environment at Digital. Sam Fuller, Dieter Huttenberger, and Dick Eckhouse also helped to make the residency a success. At Washington, Guy Almes, Ed Lazowska, and John Bennett provided helpful reviews of early drafts of this work. Finally, I would like to thank Sandy Kaplan for her technical assistance, encouragement, patience, and humor that made the writing process more enjoyable.

Contents

1 *Capability- and Object-Based System Concepts*   *1*

Capability-Based Systems   3
Memory Addressing in Computer Systems   5
The Context of an Address   9
Protection in Computer Systems   10
The Object-Based Approach   13
Capabilities and Object-Based Systems   15
Summary   17
For Further Reading   18

2 *Early Descriptor Architectures*   *21*

Introduction   21
The Burroughs B5000   22
The Rice University Computer   25
The Basic Language Machine   30
Discussion   34
For Further Reading   38

3 *Early Capability Architectures*   *41*

Introduction   41
Dennis and Van Horn's Supervisor   41
The MIT PDP-1 Timesharing System   47
The Chicago Magic Number Machine   48
The CAL-TSS System   52
Discussion   57
For Further Reading   61

4 *The Plessey System 250*   *65*

Introduction   65

System Overview 66
Capability Addressing 66
Capability Register Usage 69
Inform and Outform Capabilities 69
Instructions and Addressing 71
Protected Procedure Calls 72
Operating System Resource Management 73
Input and Output 74
Discussion 75
For Further Reading 77

5 *The Cambridge CAP Computer*   *79*
Introduction 79
Hardware Overview 79
CAP Process Structure 80
CAP Addressing Overview 81
Capabilities and Virtual Addresses 83
Process Data Structures 85
Memory Address Evaluation 86
Subprocess Creation 87
The Capability Unit 89
Protected Procedures 90
Long-Term Storage and Long-Term Names 95
Discussion 96
For Further Reading 99

6 *The Hydra System*   *103*
Introduction 103
Hydra Overview 103
Hydra Objects and Types 105
Processes, Procedures, and Local Name Spaces 107
Hydra Operations 109
Capabilities and Rights 111
Supporting Protected Subsystems 113
   Templates 113
   Typecalls 116
Hydra Object Storage System 116
Capability Representation 120
Reference Counts and Garbage Collection 121
Discussion 122
For Further Reading 125

7 *The STAROS System*   *127*
Overview of STAROS 127
STAROS Object Support 129

STArOS Capabilities   130
Object Addressing   131
STArOS Abstract Type Management   133
Discussion   134
For Further Reading   135

8   *The IBM System/38*   *137*

Introduction   137
System Objects   139
Object Addressing   141
  Virtual Memory   141
  Pointers   142
  Contexts   144
  Physical Address Mapping   145
Profiles and Authority   147
  Authority/Pointer Resolution   148
Programs/Procedures   150
  The Instruction Stream   151
  Program Activation and Invocation   152
  Protected Procedures   153
Special Privileges   154
Discussion   154
For Further Reading   157

9   *The Intel iAPX 432*   *159*

Introduction   159
Segments and Objects   161
Object Addressing   163
  Object Descriptors   163
  Access Descriptors   165
Program Execution   167
  Domains and Instruction Objects   168
  Procedure Call and Context Objects   169
  Instruction Operand Addressing   171
  Context Allocation   172
  Parameter Passing   173
Abstraction Support   173
  Domains and Refinements   174
  Creation of Typed Objects   176
  Programmer-Defined Types   177
Storage Resources   179
Instructions   182
Discussion   184
For Further Reading   186

10 *Issues in Capability-Based Architectures* *187*

Introduction 187
Segmentation 188
Storage of Capabilities 189
Capability Representation 191
Objects 195
Protected Procedures and Type Extension 196
Object Lifetimes and Garbage Collection 197
Object Locking 201
Revocation 202
Conclusions 203

Capability and Object System Bibliography *205*

Index *217*

Figures

1-1. A Capability *3*
1-2. Conventional Segment Address Translation *6*
1-3. Capability Register Addressing *7*
1-4. System Object Access Matrix *11*
1-5. Access Control and Capability Lists *11*

2-1. B5000 Program Reference Table *23*
2-2. B5000 Descriptor Formats *24*
2-3. Rice University Computer Codeword Format *27*
2-4. Rice University Computer Memory Organization *29*
2-5. Example of BLM Numeric Formats *32*
2-6. Basic Language Machine Addressing *33*
2-7. BLM Address and Codeword Formats *34*

3-1. Processes, Computations, and C-lists *43*
3-2. Protected Procedure Protection Spheres *46*
3-3. Chicago Magic Number Machine Linkage Segment *52*
3-4. CAL-TSS Object Addressing *55*

4-1. Plessey System 250 Capability Formats *67*
4-2. Plessey System 250 Capability Loading *68*
4-3. System 250 Instruction Formats *71*
4-4. Protected Procedure Resource Subsystem *74*

5-1. CAP Process Hierarchy *81*
5-2. CAP Process Addressing *82*
5-3. CAP Capability and Access Rights Formats *83*
5-4. CAP Virtual Address *84*
5-5. CAP PRL Entry *85*
5-6. CAP Process Base *86*

5-7. Capability Unit Register Format *89*

5-8. CAP Capability Unit *91*

5-9. CAP Enter Capability and Enter PRL Formats *92*

5-10. CAP Protected Object Implementation *94*

6-1. Hydra Object and Type Object *106*

6-2. Hydra Type Hierarchy *108*

6-3. Hydra Capability *111*

6-4. Hydra Procedure Call *115*

6-5. Hydra TypeCall *117*

6-6. Active Fixed Part Directory *119*

6-7. Hydra Capability Formats *121*

7-1. A CM★ Cluster *128*

7-2. StarOS Capability and Capability Rights Word *130*

7-3. StarOS Object Descriptor Format *132*

7-4. StarOS Directory Structure *133*

8-1. System/38 Implementation Layers *138*

8-2. IBM System/38 System Object *140*

8-3. System/38 Virtual Address *142*

8-4. System/38 Virtual Address Translation *146*

8-5. System/38 Example High-level Instruction *152*

9-1. Intel iAPX 432 Structure *160*

9-2. Intel 432 Segment *161*

9-3. Intel 432 Storage Segment Descriptor *163*

9-4. Intel 432 Access Descriptor *165*

9-5. Intel 432 Address Translation *167*

9-6. Intel 432 Domain and Instruction Objects *168*

9-7. Intel 432 Context Object Representation *170*

9-8. Intel 432 Access Selector Formats *172*

9-9. Intel 432 Parameter Passing *174*

9-10. Intel 432 Domain Refinement *175*

9-11. Intel 432 Type Control Object Data Part *176*

9-12. Intel 432 Dynamic Object Addressing *178*

9-13. Intel 432 Storage Resource Object *179*

9-14. Intel 432 Instruction Format *182*

9-15. Intel 432 Reference Format *183*

Tables

1-1. Major Descriptor and Capability Systems *2*

3-1. Dennis and Van Horn Supervisor Capability Operations *44*

3-2. Chicago Magic Number Supervisor Capability Operations *51*

6-1. Hydra Kernel-Implemented Types *107*
6-2. Generic Object and Capability Operations *110*
6-3. Capability and Generic Object Access Rights *111*
6-4. Hydra Active and Passive Fixed Parts *118*

7-1. STAROS Representation Types *129*
7-2. STAROS Capability Types *131*

8-1. System/38 System Object Types *139*
8-2. System/38 Pointer Instructions *144*
8-3. System/38 Context Instructions *145*
8-4. System/38 Authority Management Instructions *149*

9-1. Intel 432 System Object Types *162*
9-2. Intel 432 Storage Segment Descriptor Fields *164*
9-3. Intel 432 Access Descriptor Instructions *166*

Capability-Based Computer Systems

Capability- and Object-Based System Concepts

Although the complexity of computer applications increases yearly, the underlying hardware architecture for applications has remained unchanged for decades. It is, therefore, not surprising that the demands of modern applications have exposed limitations in conventional architectures. For example, many conventional systems lack support in:

1. *Information sharing and communications.* An essential system function is the dynamic sharing and exchange of information, whether on a timesharing system or across a network. Fundamental to the sharing of storage is the addressing or naming of objects. Sharing is difficult on conventional systems because addressing is local to a single process. Sharing would be simplified if addresses could be transmitted between processes and used to access the shared data.

2. *Protection and security.* As information sharing becomes easier, users require access controls on their private data. It must also be possible to share information with, or run programs written by, other users without compromising confidential data. On conventional systems, all of a user's objects are accessible to any program which the user runs. Protection would be enhanced if a user could restrict access to only those objects a program requires for its execution.

3. *Reliable construction and maintenance of complex systems.* Conventional architectures support a single privileged mode of operation. This structure leads to monolithic design; any module needing protection must be part of the single operating system kernel. If, instead, any module could execute within a protected domain, systems could be built as a collection of independent modules extensible by any user.

Over the last several decades, computer industry and university scientists have been searching for alternative architectures that better support these essential functions. One alternative architectural structure is *capability-based* addressing. Capability-based systems support the *object-based* approach to computing.

This book explains the capability/object-based approach and its implications, and examines the features, advantages, and disadvantages of many existing designs. Each chapter presents details of one or more capability-based systems. Table 1-1 lists the systems described, where they were developed, and when they were designed or introduced.

System	Developer	Year	Attributes
Rice University Computer	Rice University	1959	segmented memory with "codeword" addressing
Burroughs B5000	Burroughs Corp.	1961	stack machine with descriptor addressing
Basic Language Machine	International Computers Ltd., U.K.	1964	high-level machine with codeword addressing
Dennis and Van Horn Supervisor	MIT	1966	conceptual design for capability supervisor
PDP-1 Time-sharing System	MIT	1967	capability supervisor
Multicomputer/ Magic Number Machine	University of Chicago Institute for Computer Research	1967	first capability hardware system design
CAL-TSS	U.C. Berkeley Computer Center	1968	capability operating system for CDC 6400
System 250	Plessey Corp., U.K.	1969	first industrial capability hardware and software system
CAP Computer	University of Cambridge, U.K.	1970	capability hardware with microcode support
Hydra	Carnegie-Mellon University	1971	object-based multi-processor O.S.
StarOS	Carnegie-Mellon University	1975	object-based multi-processor O.S.
System/38	IBM, Rochester, MN.	1978	first major commercial capability system, tagged capabilities
iAPX 432	Intel, Aloha, OR.	1981	highly-integrated object-based micro-processor system

Table 1-1: Major Descriptor and Capability Systems

Before surveying these systems at a detailed architectural level, it is useful to introduce the concepts of capabilities and object-based systems. This chapter defines the concept of capability, describes the use of capabilities in memory addressing and protection, introduces the object-based programming approach, and relates object-based systems to capability-based addressing.

Simplified examples of capability-based and conventional computer systems are presented throughout this chapter. These examples are meant to introduce the capability model by contrasting it with more traditional addressing mechanisms. In fact, many design choices are possible in both domains, and many conventional systems exhibit some of the properties of capability systems. No one of the following models is representative of all capability or conventional systems.

1.1 Capability-Based Systems

Capability-based systems differ significantly from conventional computer systems. Capabilities provide (1) a single mechanism to address both primary and secondary memory, and (2) a single mechanism to address both hardware and software resources. While solving many difficult problems in complex system design, capability systems introduce new challenges of their own.

Conceptually, a capability is a token, ticket, or key that gives the possessor permission to access an entity or object in a computer system. A capability is implemented as a data structure that contains two items of information: a *unique object identifier* and *access rights*, as shown in Figure 1-1.

The identifier *addresses* or *names* a single object in the computer system. An object, in this context, can be any logical or physical entity, such as a segment of memory, an array, a file, a

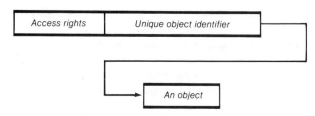

Figure 1-1: A Capability

line printer, or a message port. The access rights define the *operations* that can be performed on that object. For example, the access rights can permit read-only access to a memory segment or send-and-receive access to a message port.

Each user, program, or procedure in a capability system has access to a *list of capabilities*. These capabilities identify all of the objects which that user, program, or procedure is permitted to access. To specify an object, the user provides the *index* of a capability in the list. For example, to output a record to a file, the user might call the file system as follows:

PUT(file_capability , "this is a record");

The capability specified in the call serves two purposes. First, it identifies the file to be written. Second, it indicates whether the operation to be performed (PUT in this case) is permitted.

A capability thus provides addressing and access rights to an object. Capabilities are the basis for object protection; a program cannot access an object unless its capability list contains a suitably privileged capability for the object. Therefore, the system must prohibit a program from directly modifying the bits in a capability. If a program could modify the bits in a capability, it could forge access to any object in the system by changing the identifier and access rights fields.

Capability system integrity is usually maintained by prohibiting direct program modification of the capability list. The capability list is modified only by the operating system or the hardware. However, programs can obtain new capabilities by executing operating system or hardware operations. For example, when a program calls an operating system routine to create a new file, the operating system stores a capability for that file in the program's capability list. A capability system also provides other capability operations. Examples include operations to:

1. Move capabilities to different locations in a capability list.
2. Delete a capability.
3. Restrict the rights in a capability, producing a less-privileged version.
4. Pass a capability as a parameter to a procedure.
5. Transmit a capability to another user in the system.

Thus, a program can execute direct control over the movement of capabilities and can share capabilities, and therefore, objects, with other programs and users.

It is possible for a user to have several capability lists. One list will generally be the master capability list containing capabilities for secondary lists, and so on. This structure is similar to a multi-level directory system, but, while directories address only files, capabilities address objects of many types.

1.1.1 Memory Addressing in Computer Systems

This section presents simplified models for both conventional and capability-based memory addressing systems. Although capabilities can control access to many object types, early capability-based systems concentrated on using capabilities for primary memory addressing. The first use of capabilities for memory protection was in the Chicago Magic Number Machine [Fabry 67, Yngve 68], and an early description of capability-based memory protection appeared in Wilkes' book on timesharing systems [Wilkes 68]. Later, [Fabry 74] described the advantages of capabilities for generalized addressing and sharing.

For purposes of a simplified model, consider a conventional computer supporting a multiprogramming system in which each program executes within a single process. A program is divided into a collection of segments, where a segment is a contiguous section of memory that represents some logical entity, such as a procedure or array. A process defines a program's address space: that is, the memory segments it can access. The process also contains data structures that describe the user, and a directory that contains the names of a set of files. These files represent the user's long-term storage.

When a program is run, the operating system creates a process-local segment table that defines the memory segments available to the program. The segment table is a list of *descriptors* that contain physical information about each segment. Figure 1-2 shows example formats for a process virtual address and segment table descriptor. The operating system loads various segments needed by the program into primary memory, and loads the segment table descriptors with the physical address and length of each segment. A process can then access segments by reading from or writing to virtual addresses.

Each virtual address contains two fields: the segment number and the offset of a memory element within that specified segment. On each virtual address reference the hardware uses the segment number field as an index to locate an entry in the

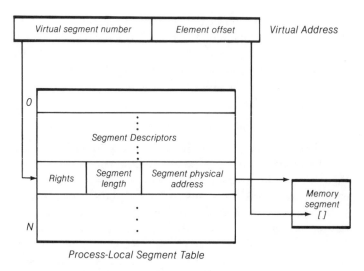

Process-Local Segment Table

Figure 1-2: Conventional Segment Address Translation

process segment table. This descriptor contains the physical location of the segment. The length field in the descriptor is used to check that the offset in the virtual address is within the segment bounds. The rights field in the segment table entry indicates the type of access permitted to that segment (for example, read or write).

The model shown in Figure 1-2 has the following properties:

1. The system supports a segmented process virtual address space. A virtual address is local to the process and is translated through the process-local segment table.

2. A program can construct any virtual address and can attempt to read or write that address. On each reference, the hardware ensures that (a) the segment exists, (b) the offset is valid, and (c) the attempted operation is permitted. Otherwise, an error is signaled.

3. Loading of segment table entries is a privileged operation and can be accomplished only by the operating system. In general, a segment table is created at the time a program is loaded. The program then executes in a static addressing environment.

4. Sharing of segments between processes requires that the operating system arrange for both process-local segment tables to address the shared segments. If two processes wish to use the same virtual address to access a shared segment,

the segment descriptors must be in the same locations in both segment tables.

5. Any dynamic sharing of segments requires operating system intervention to load segment descriptors.

A *capability-based system* also supports the concept of a process that defines a program's execution environment. In the capability system, each process has a capability list that defines the segments it can access. Instead of the segment table descriptors available to the conventional system hardware, the capability addressing system consists of a set of *capability registers*. The *program* can execute hardware instructions to transfer capabilities between the capability list and the capability registers. The number of capability registers is generally small compared to the size of the capability list. Thus, at any time, the capability registers define a subset of the potentially accessible segments that can be physically addressed by the hardware. A simplified hardware model for this system is shown in Figure 1-3.

The model shown in Figure 1-3 has the following properties:

1. The system has a segmented virtual address space. A segment of memory can only be addressed by an instruction if a capability for that segment has been loaded into a capability register.

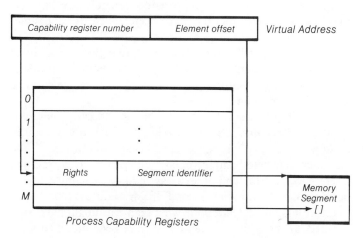

Figure 1-3: Capability Register Addressing

7

2. While loading of a segment descriptor in the conventional system is privileged, loading of a capability register is not. Instead of controlling the loading of the register, the capability system controls *the pattern of bits* that can be loaded. Only a valid capability can be loaded into a capability register.

3. The capability system provides a dynamically changing address space. The address space changes whenever the program changes one of the capability registers.

4. A virtual address identifies a process-local capability register. In this sense, a virtual address has similar properties to a virtual address in the conventional system. Sharing a virtual address does not in itself give access to the same segment.

5. A capability, however, is *not* process-local. Capabilities are *context independent*; that is, the segment addressed by a capability is independent of the process using that capability. A process can share a segment by copying or sending a capability from its capability list to the capability list of a cooperating process. Each of the processes can then access the segment.

One important difference between the conventional and capability approaches involves the ability of a program to affect system-wide or process-local objects. In the conventional system, a program executes within a virtual address space defined by a process. Every procedure called by that program has access to the process address space, including segments and files. Every procedure executes within an identical protection environment.

In the capability system, a procedure can only affect objects for which capability registers have been loaded. It is possible, therefore, for different procedures called by the same program to have access to different segments. Although all procedures may have the potential to load capability registers from the capability list, some procedures may choose to execute within a very small addressing sphere.

The ability to restrict the execution or addressing environment of a procedure has several benefits. First, if a procedure is allowed access only to those segments absolutely needed, the hardware can detect any erroneous references. For example, a reference past the end of an array might be caught before it destroys another variable. Second, if a procedure is found to be in error, it is easy to determine what segments might have been affected. If the segments that could have been modified were local to the procedure, recovery might be substantially easier.

Most capability systems go a step further by allowing each procedure to have a *private* capability list. A procedure can thus protect its objects from accidental or malicious access by its callers, and a program can protect its objects from access by called procedures. Every procedure can have, in effect, its own address space. To permit a procedure access to a local object, a program can pass a capability for the object as a parameter when the procedure is called. Therefore, in a capability system, every procedure can be protected from every other procedure because each has a private capability list. When one procedure calls another, it knows that the called procedure can access only local objects for which capabilities are passed.

1.1.2 The Context of an Address

Each object in a capability system has a unique identifier. Conceptually, each object's identifier is unique for all time. That is, an identifier is assigned when an object is created and that identifier is never reused, even after the object is deleted. During the object's lifetime, its unique identifier is used within capabilities to specify the object. An attempt to use a capability with an identifier for a deleted object causes an error.

In practice, the object identifier field of a capability must be used by hardware to locate the object. From the hardware viewpoint, the identifier is an address—either the address of a segment or perhaps the address of a central descriptor that contains physical information about the segment. The need to handle addresses efficiently in hardware typically causes addresses to be small—16 or 32 bits, for example. For this reason, identifiers tend to have too few bits to be unique for all time. However, the choice of the number of bits in an identifier is an important system design decision that dictates the way in which capabilities can be used.

In conventional systems, an address is meaningful only within a single process. In a capability system, addresses (capabilities and their identifiers) are context-independent. That is, the interpretation of a capability is independent of the process using it. The unique identifier within a capability must have a system-wide interpretation. Unique identifiers must be large enough to address all of the segments likely to be in use by all executing processes at any time. This allows capabilities to be freely passed between processes and used to access shared data.

Addressing on most conventional systems is restricted in terms of time as well as context. An address is meaningful only within the lifetime of a single process. Therefore, addresses cannot be used to name objects whose lifetimes are greater than

9

the process creating the objects. If a process wishes to create a long-term storage object, such as a file, it must interface to the file system. Files typically require different naming, protection, and storage mechanisms than memory segments.

A significant advance made possible by capabilities is the naming and protection of both long-term and short-term objects with a single mechanism. If the identifier field is very large, it may be possible to implement identifiers unique for all time. Each object is addressed by capabilities containing its unique identifier, independent of whether it is stored in primary or secondary memory. The operating system or hardware can maintain data structures that indicate the location of each object. If a program attempts to access an object in secondary memory, the hardware or operating system can bring the object into primary memory so that the operation can be completed. From the program's point of view, however, there is a single-level address space. Capabilities, as well as data, can be saved for long periods of time and stored in secondary memory.

There are, therefore, several contexts in which an address can have meaning. For example, for:

1. Primary memory segments of a single process.
2. Primary memory segments of all existing processes.
3. All existing segments in both primary and secondary memory.

Most conventional systems support only type 1, while capabilities allow for any of the listed addressing types. More importantly, while conventional systems are concerned only with the protection of *data*, capability systems are concerned also with the protection of *addresses*. A process on a capability system cannot fabricate new addresses. As systems become more general in their addressing structure as in types 2 and 3, the protection of addresses becomes crucial to the integrity of the system.

1.1.3 Protection in Computer Systems

Lampson contrasts the capability approach with the traditional approach by showing the structure of protection information needed in a traditional operating system [Lampson 71]. Figure 1-4 depicts an access matrix showing the privileges that each system user is permitted with respect to each system object. For example, user Fred has read and write privileges to File1 and no privileges to File2, while user Sandy is allowed to read both files.

	File1	File2	File3	ProcessJ	Mailbox10	...
Fred	Read Write		Read	Delete Suspend Wakeup	Send	
Sandy	Read	Read			Send Receive	
Molly			Read Write		Send	
. . .						

System Users (label at left, spanning Fred/Sandy/Molly rows)

Figure 1-4: System Object Access Matrix

One conventional approach to the maintenance of protection information is *access control lists*, in which the operating system keeps an *access list* for each object in the system. Each object's list contains the names of users permitted access to the object and the privileges they may exercise. When a user attempts to access an object, the operating system checks the access list associated with that object to see if the operation is authorized. Each of the columns of Figure 1-4 represents an access control list.

The capability system offers an alternative structure in which the operating system arranges protection information by user instead of by object. A *capability list* is associated with each user in the system. Each capability contains the name of an object in the system and the user's permitted privileges for accessing the object. To access an object, the user specifies a capability in the local capability list. Each of the rows of Figure 1-4 represents a capability list. Figure 1-5 shows an access list

Access List for Mailbox10	*Capability list for Fred*
Fred(send)	File1(read,write)
Sandy(send,receive)	File3(read)
Molly(send)	ProcessJ(delete,suspend,wakeup)
.	Mailbox10(send)
.	.
.	.
	.

Figure 1-5: Access Control and Capability Lists

and a capability list derived from the protection matrix in Figure 1-4.

One important difference between the capability list and access list is the user's ability to *name* objects. In the access list approach, a user can attempt to name any object in the system as the target of an operation. The system then checks that object's access list. In the capability system, however, a user can only name those objects for which a capability is held: that is, to which some access is permitted.

In either case, the integrity of the system is only as good as the integrity of the data structures used to maintain the protection information. Both access control list and capability list mechanisms must be carefully controlled so that users cannot gain unauthorized access to an object.

Similar protection options exist outside the computer world. A useful analogy is the control of a safe deposit box. Suppose, for example, that Carla wishes to keep all of her valuables in a safe deposit box in the bank. On occasion, she would like one or more trustworthy friends to make deposits or withdrawals. There are basically two ways that the bank can control access to the box. First, the bank can maintain a list of people authorized to access the box. To make a transaction, Carla or any of her friends must prove their identity to the bank's satisfaction. The bank checks the (access control) list for Carla's safe deposit box and allows the transaction if the person is authorized. Or, instead of maintaining a list, the bank can issue Carla one or more keys to her safe deposit box. If Carla needs to have a friend access the box, she simply gives a key to the friend.

A number of observations can be made about these two alternative protection systems. The properties of the access list scheme are:

1. The bank must maintain a list for each safe deposit box.
2. The bank must ensure the validity of the list at all times (e.g., it cannot allow the night watchman to add a name).
3. The bank must be able to verify the identity of those asking to use a box.
4. To allow a new person to use the box, the owner must visit the bank, verify that he or she is the owner of the box, and have the new name added to the list.
5. A friend cannot extend his or her privilege to someone else.
6. If a friend becomes untrustworthy, the owner can visit the bank and have that person's name removed from the list.

The alternative scheme involving keys has the following properties:

1. The bank need not be involved in any transactions once the keys are given, except to allow a valid keyholder into the vault.
2. The physical lock and key system must be relatively secure; that is, it must be extremely difficult to forge a key or to pick the lock on a safe deposit box.
3. The owner of a box can simply pass a key to anyone who needs to access the box.
4. Once a key has been passed to a friend, it is difficult to keep them from giving the key to someone else.
5. Once a friend has made a transaction, the owner can ask for the key back, although it may not be possible to know whether or not the friend has made a copy.

The advantage of the key-based system is ease of use for both the bank and customer. However, if today's friends are likely to become tomorrow's enemies, the access list has the advantage of simple guaranteed access removal. Of course, the access control list and the key (or capability) systems are not mutually exclusive, and can be combined in either the computer or banking world to provide the advantages of both systems for increased protection.

1.2 The Object-Based Approach

Over the last few decades, several areas of computer science have converged on a single approach to system design. This approach, known as *object-based computing*, seeks to raise the level of abstraction in system design. The events that have encouraged object-based design include:

1. Advances in computer architecture, including capability systems and hardware support for operating systems concepts.
2. Advances in programming languages, as demonstrated in Simula [Dahl 66], Pascal [Jensen 75], Smalltalk [Ingalls 78], CLU [Liskov 77], and Ada [DOD 80].
3. Advances in programming methodology, including modularization and information hiding [Parnas 72] and monitors [Hoare 74].

This section introduces the object approach and discusses its relationship to capability-based computer systems.

What is object-based computing? Simply stated, the object approach is a method of structuring systems that supports *ab-*

straction. It is a philosophy of system design that decomposes a problem into (1) a set of *abstract object types*, or resources in the system, and (2) a set of *operations* that manipulate *instances* of each object type.

To make this idea more concrete, consider the following simplified example. Imagine that we are programming a traffic simulation for a city. First, define a set of objects that represent, abstractly, the fundamental entities that make up the traffic system. Some of the object *types* for the traffic simulation might be:

- passenger
- bus
- bus stop
- taxi
- car

Then, for each object type, define the operations that can be performed. Bus objects, for example, might support the operations:

- PUT_BUS_INTO_SERVICE(bus_number)
- MOVE_BUS(bus_number, bus_stop)
- LOAD_PASSENGERS(bus_number, passenger_list)
- UNLOAD_PASSENGERS(bus_number, passenger_list)
- GET_PASSENGER_COUNT(bus_number)
- GET_POSITION(bus_number)
- REMOVE_BUS_FROM_SERVICE(bus_number)

Each bus operation accepts a bus number as a parameter. At any time there may be many bus objects in the system, and we identify each bus by a unique number. Each of these bus objects is an *instance* of the *type* bus. The *type* of an object identifies it as a member of a class of objects that share some behavioral properties, such as the set of operations that can be performed on them.

What has been gained by defining the system in this way? First, there now exist a fundamental set of objects and operations for the simulation. We can now implement the procedures to perform the operations on each type of object. Since only a limited number of procedures operate on each object type, access to the internal data structures used to maintain the state of each type can be restricted. This isolation of the knowledge of those data structures should simplify any future

changes to one of the object abstractions because only a limited
set of procedures is affected.

Second, and more importantly, we have raised the *level of
abstraction* in the simulation program. That is, we can now
program the simulation using buses, passengers, and bus stops
as the fundamental objects, instead of bits, bytes, and words,
which are normally provided by the underlying hardware. The
buses and passengers are our data types just as bits and bytes
are the data types supported in hardware. The simulation program will consist mainly of control structures plus procedure
calls to perform operations on instances of our fundamental
objects.

Of course, in this example, the procedures implementing
the operations are programmed using lower-level objects, such
as bytes, words, and so on. Or, they may be further decom-
posed into simpler abstract objects that are then implemented
at a low level. Object-based systems provide a fundamental set
of objects that can be used for computing. From this basis, the
programmer constructs new higher-level object types using
combinations of the fundamental objects. In this way the system is extended to provide new features by creating more sophisticated abstractions.

This methodology aims to increase productivity, improve
reliability, and ease system modification. Through the use of
well-defined and well-controlled object interfaces, systems designers hope to simplify the construction of complex computer
systems.

1.2.1 Capabilities and Object-Based Systems

In the simulation example, each object is identified by a
unique number. To move a bus from one stop to another, we
call the MOVE_BUS operation with the unique number of the
bus to move. For purposes of the simple simulation, a small set
of integers suffices to identify the buses or other objects. No
protection is needed because these objects are implemented
and used by a single program.

The use of the object approach to build operating system
facilities presents different requirements. For example, suppose we wish to build a calendar system to keep track of scheduled meetings, deadlines, reminders, and so on. The fundamental object of the calendar system, from the user's point of
view, is a calendar object. Our calendar management system
provides routines that create a new calendar, and modify,

15

query, or display an existing calendar. Many users in the system will, of course, want to use this facility.

Several familiar issues now arise: (1) how does a user name a calendar object, (2) how is that calendar protected from access by other users, and (3) how can calendars be shared under controlled circumstances? Only the owner of a calendar should be able to make changes, and the annotations in each calendar must be protected from other users, since they might contain confidential information. However, a user might permit selected other users to check if he or she is busy during a certain time, in order to automate the scheduling of meetings.

Capabilities provide a solution to these problems. When a user creates a new calendar, the calendar creation routine allocates a segment of memory for which it receives a capability. This segment is used to store data structures that will hold the calendar's state. The create routine uses this capability to initialize the data structures, and then returns it to the caller as proof of ownership of the calendar. In order to later modify or query the calendar, the user specifies the returned capability; the capability identifies the calendar and allows the modify or query procedure to gain access to the data structures. Only a user with a valid capability can access a calendar.

A weakness with this scenario is that the calendar system cannot prevent the calendar owner from using its capability to access the data structures directly. The calendar system would like to protect its data structures both to ensure consistency and to guarantee that future changes in data format are invisible outside of the subsystem. In addition, if a user passes a calendar capability to another user, the second user can then modify the data structures or read confidential information.

These problems exist because the calendar system returns a fully-privileged calendar capability to the user. Instead, what is needed is a capability that identifies a specific calendar and is proof of ownership, but does not allow direct access to the underlying data structures. In other words, the calendar system would like to return only *restricted* capabilities to its clients. However, the calendar system must retain the ability to later *amplify* the privileges in one of its restricted capabilities so that it can access the data structures for a calendar.

There are several ways of providing type managers with this special ability. (These mechanisms are examined in detail throughout the book.) However, given this power over capabilities for its objects, a type manager can ensure that its clients operate only through the well-defined object operation interface. A client can pass a capability parameter to the type manager when requesting a service, but cannot otherwise use the capability to read or write the object it addresses. This facility is fundamental to any system that allows creation and protection of new system types.

1.3 Summary

The capability concept can be applied in hardware and software to many problems in computer system design. Capabilities provide a different way of thinking about addressing, protection, and sharing of objects. Some of the properties of capabilities illustrated in this chapter include their use in:

1. Addressing primary memory in a computer system.
2. Sharing objects.
3. Providing a uniform means of addressing short- and long-term storage.
4. Support for a dynamic addressing environment.
5. Support for data abstraction and information hiding.

These, of course, are advantages of capability-based systems. The most important advantage is support for object-based programming. Object-based programming methodology seeks to simplify the design, implementation, debugging, and maintenance of sophisticated applications. While capabilities solve a number of system problems, their use raises a whole new set of concerns. And, as is often the case in computer system design, the concept is much simpler than the implementation.

The remainder of this book is devoted to examining many different capability-based and object-based designs. The characteristics of each system are described with emphasis on addressing, protection, and object management. Each system represents a different set of tradeoffs and presents different advantages and disadvantages. When comparing the systems, consider the differences in goals, technologies, and resources available to the system developers.

The final chapter of this book considers issues in capability system design common to all of the systems described. A few of the questions to be considered follow. It may be useful to remember these questions when examining each system design.

1. What is the structure of an address?
2. How is a capability represented? How is a capability used to locate an object?

3. How are capabilities protected?
4. What is the lifetime of a capability?
5. What types of objects are supported by the hardware and software?
6. What is the lifetime of an object?
7. How can users extend the primitive set of objects provided by the base hardware and software?

1.4 For Further Reading

The concept of capability is formally defined in the 1966 paper by Dennis and Van Horn [Dennis 66]. Chapter 3 examines this paper in some detail. The paper by Fabry [Fabry 74] compares capability addressing and conventional segmented addressing of primary memory, while Redell [Redell 74a] describes issues in capability systems and the use of sealing mechanisms that support the addition of new object types to a system. These papers are a fundamental part of capability literature.

Capability systems have been discussed in various contexts. Two papers by Lampson [Lampson 69 and Lampson 71] describe the requirements for protection in operating systems and the capability protection model. The surveys by Linden [Linden 76] and Denning [Denning 76], which appeared in a special issue of *ACM Computing Surveys*, describe capability systems and their relationship to security and fault tolerance in operating systems.

The architecture books by Myers [Myers 82] and Iliffe [Iliffe 82] also discuss some of the systems described in this book. Myers' book contains details of Sward [Myers 80], a capability-based research system built at IBM that is omitted here. A capability system model, as well as discussion of some existing capability systems, appears in the book by Gehringer [Gehringer 82]. Jones [Jones 78a] provides a good introduction to the concepts of object-based programming.

The Burroughs B5000 computer. (Courtesy Burroughs Corporation.)

Early Descriptor Architectures

2.1 Introduction

During the late 1950s and early 1960s a host of architectural experiments attacked significant problems in computer system utilization. Most computers of that era were batch systems that ran one program at a time. A program was loaded into a contiguous section of primary memory and run until completion; then another program was loaded and run. This static execution and memory environment made inefficient use of the costly processor, memory, and peripherals. In addition, programs had little flexibility for meeting dynamic programming demands.

Multiprogramming systems showed increased processor utilization as long as several runnable programs could be kept in primary memory. However, multiprogramming required more sophisticated memory management techniques and forced operating systems to deal with dynamic storage allocation and compaction. These tasks were greatly eased by the introduction of paged systems in which all storage units were the same size.

Although paging helped the operating system to manage storage, it did little to help the programmer with the task of programming. A program still had to manage a conventional linear address space. It was difficult to protect instructions or data separately, to catch array bounds violations, to increase the size of arrays and other data structures dynamically, or to create new data structures dynamically.

The concept of segmentation, however, aided both the programmer and the operating system. A segment is a contiguous section of memory that represents some logical entity, such as a procedure or array. The programmer views memory as a collection of segments, each separately addressable. A program addresses each memory element by a segment number and the offset of that element within the specified segment. Because each segment has a size, array bounds violations can be caught by placing the array within a single segment.

An operating system can load each segment into memory separately or relocate segments if needed (for example, to enlarge the size of the segment). However, for an operating system to manipulate segments easily, it must ensure that physical memory addresses are not embedded in the program. The simplest way to isolate the program from its physical memory location is to provide a level of indirection between program-generated addresses and the primary memory addresses of data elements. Just as page tables provide this indirection in the paged virtual memory system, segment descriptors—or segment base/limit registers in some hardware implementations—provide the indirection in a segmented system. A segment descriptor is a data element that contains the primary memory address and size of a segment. An operating system need only modify the relevant descriptors when relocating segments.

This chapter examines several early descriptor-based computer designs: the Burroughs B5000, the Rice University Computer, and the Basic Language Machine. Although these systems preceded the formal definition of capability, each system implemented capability-like structures in its addressing mechanisms. These machines were distinguished from their contemporaries by the generalized way in which they applied the concept of descriptor.

2.2 The Burroughs B5000

Much of the innovation in commercial computer architectures in the early 1960s emanated from the Burroughs Corporation. Introduced in 1961, the Burroughs B5000 system had several features unique for its time [Burroughs 61]. Most important was the use of segmentation for structuring memory and the use of descriptors for addressing segments. Also, the B5000 was geared to execute high-level language programs, particularly ALGOL and COBOL. In fact, assembly language was not available to the user. The system was designed to compile and execute high-level languages efficiently, and relied on a stack-oriented instruction set to aid in expression evaluation and procedure activation. The B5000 supported multiprocessing as well as multiprogramming by allowing connection of two processing units.

On the B5000 a program consists of many data segments and code segments. Each executing program has a local addressing environment consisting of its memory segments, its private stack, and a private *Program Reference Table* (PRT). The Program Reference Table, up to 1024 48-bit words in length, contains *descriptors* that locate the user's code and data segments in memory, and *values* of scalar elements, as shown in Figure 2-1. A *tag* field in each word in the table indicates whether the entry is a descriptor or a scalar data element. All memory references, including procedure calls, are made through Program Reference Table descriptors; thus, the Program Reference Table completely defines the domain of execution for each user program. When a program is running, a hardware register holds the address of its Program Reference Table.

The B5000 supports three different descriptor types: data descriptors, program descriptors, and input/output descriptors. The formats of these descriptors are shown in Figure 2-2. *Data descriptors* contain the size, primary memory address, and drum unit number and address of a data segment. *Program descriptors* are allocated for each procedure and every segment of the main program. Reference to a program descriptor automatically causes a procedure call. *Input/output descriptors* are

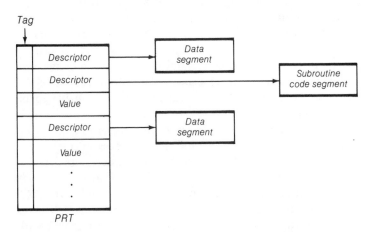

Figure 2-1: B5000 Program Reference Table

Tag	P	Drum number	Segment size	Drum address	Memory address

Data and Program Descriptor

Tag	P	Unit number	Operation size	Operation type	Format/ control	Memory address

I/O Descriptor

Figure 2-2: B5000 Descriptor Formats

command words for the operating system, specifying the size and type of transfer and any special device control or formatting information. The operating system selects a physical unit and allocates primary memory for the operation if needed.

The presence bit (P) in data and program descriptors indicates whether or not the segment is currently in primary memory. If reference is made to a segment not in primary memory, a trap occurs and the operating system automatically loads the segment from drum.

The B5000 is a stack machine and all instructions operate on the stack. The stack is stored in memory; however, the top two stack elements are held in hardware registers called the A and B registers. As items are pushed onto the stack, they move first into the A register, then to the B register, and finally into memory as more items are pushed. As items are popped from the stack, data moves from memory into the B register. All arithmetic operations are performed on operands held in the A and B registers, leaving a single result in the B register.

Each 48-bit B5000 instruction word is divided into four 12-bit instruction *syllables*. There are four types of instruction syllables: operators, literals, operand calls, and descriptor calls. An *operator* syllable operates on the top one or two elements of the stack, leaving a single-word result. A *literal* syllable simply causes a 10-bit literal field in the syllable to be pushed on the stack.

A program executes an *operand call* syllable to load a data item onto the stack. The operand call references an entry in the Program Reference Table, with three possible results depending on the type of entry encountered. First, if the PRT entry is a scalar, the scalar is pushed onto the stack. Second, if the PRT entry contains a program descriptor, a subroutine call takes place. Third, if the entry is a descriptor for a segment with length greater than zero, then array indexing takes place as follows. The contents of the B register, which contains the array index, is validated against the length stored in the descriptor. The index is then added to the segment base address to locate the selected word in memory. The word is read from memory and loaded into the B register, replacing the index.

Descriptors can also be loaded from the PRT onto the stack. This is required, for example, to execute the STORE operator, which saves the contents of the B register in the location addressed by the A register. A *descriptor call* syllable, used to push an address onto the stack, operates in a mode similar to the operand call. If the referenced PRT entry is a scalar, a descriptor is constructed pointing to its location in the PRT. If a PRT entry contains a descriptor, the descriptor is copied to the stack, with possible address modification by an index value in the B register. Reference to a program descriptor causes a subroutine call.

B5000 subroutines execute in *subroutine mode* which provides some special syllable formats. When a subroutine is called, input parameters (as well as linkage information) are saved on the stack by the caller. A hardware register is loaded with the address of the next available stack location past the saved parameters; this is the first location used by the subroutine for its local variables. One of the subroutine mode syllables allows stack addressing relative to the register in the positive direction (to access locals) or the negative direction (to access inputs). A subroutine can also address constants stored in the subroutine code segment using a type of program counter relative addressing. References to the caller's PRT are still permitted within the subroutine.

The B5000's use of the stack, segmentation, descriptor addressing, and high-level languages made it one of the most advanced systems of its time. These features have been expanded and generalized in later Burroughs systems and have had an effect on other manufacturers' products as well. The 16-bit Hewlett-Packard 3000 [HP 72], in particular, is an outgrowth of early Burroughs B5000 ideas. More important, the B5000 Program Reference Tables and their use in addressing and separation of process address spaces directly influenced early capability thinking.

2.3 The Rice University Computer

In 1959, development of a new machine began at Rice University. Called the Rice University Computer [Iliffe 62, Jodeit

25

The Rice University computer. Jane Jodeit is seated at the control console
with Martin Graham looking on (Courtesy Dr. Martin Graham.)

68], this system was designed for the single-program environment and was never intended to support multiprogramming.
In fact, the original physical memory of the Rice machine was
only 8K 56-bit words. However, this computer—operational
until 1971—provided important experimentation with program addressing of memory.

The Rice architecture focused on several deficiencies in conventional linear address space machines. First, conventional
hardware did not support entities corresponding to high-level
programming objects. Second, for scientific problems, conventional architectures did not support the addressing of single or
multidimensional arrays. Third, dynamic growth of data structures was difficult on conventional machines. Programmers
had to code the maximum possible size of each array into their
programs, so that contiguous storage could be preallocated.
Support of ALGOL-like languages, with array size determina-
tion at block entry time, was difficult.

To solve these problems, the Rice designers chose a segmented architecture based on the use of *codewords*. Codewords
are descriptors for logical program entities; they can be stored
in the computer's memory or registers. Each program (as

15	12	1	1	1	8	15
L	I	X	p	*	K	F

F   Physical address of the segment.

K   Specifies one of eight index registers whose contents can be used to select an array element at location $F - I + (K)$.

p   Valid bit, indicates whether physical storage is allocated or not.

*   Indirect bit.

X   Specifies that the named segment contains codewords.

I   Index of the first array element (origin of the array).

L   Length of the segment in words.

Figure 2-3: Rice University Computer Codeword Format

viewed by both the programmer and the machine) consists of a collection of segments, called blocks or arrays in the Rice design. A segment contains instructions, data, or codewords and is addressed indirectly by means of a codeword. Each segment is homogeneous, and data types cannot be mixed within a single segment. A single-bit tag within each codeword is set if the addressed segment contains codewords.

In one sense, a codeword is simply a single-word descriptor used to address a segment, similar to a segment base register or Burroughs B5000 descriptor. In another sense, a codeword *names* the block of storage it addresses. The logical machine address space seen by the program on the Rice system is totally defined by a list of *principal codewords* that it can access. The actual maintenance of codewords is provided by the operating system. The basic structure of Rice codewords (omitting unused bits) is shown in Figure 2-3.

The physically addressable memory of the Rice machine is divided into several fixed regions, as defined below:

- A 64-word table for accumulators, trap addresses, boot code, etc.
- Two 64-word directories of codewords defining array blocks for the operating system and programmer, respectively. These are the principal codewords through which all other storage is reached, including the following structures.
- A 128-word stack.
- A *symbol table* defining each named global object in the system.
- A corresponding *value table* containing values for scalars and codewords for arrays named in the symbol table.

27

The remainder of memory is allocated dynamically to user programs and data, including those addressed through the value table.

Figure 2-4 shows the structure of a Rice University Computer sample procedure. Procedure instructions can address variables within the procedure segment without reference to codewords (that is, relative to the program counter). However, external arrays, procedures, and variables are addressed through linkage words stored at the end of the procedure segment. When a procedure is compiled, the linkage words are initialized with the names of the global variables to be addressed. At procedure load time, the operating system locates the names in the symbol table and modifies the linkage words to point to the corresponding entries in the value table.

A value table entry can be a value if the object is scalar, or a codeword if it is an array, requiring one or more additional levels of indirection. Indirection is possible through a tree of codewords, and each successive level can specify one of eight index registers. For example, in addressing the two-dimensional array (2DArray) shown in Figure 2-4, each codeword in the secondary codeword segment addresses one row of the array. Indirection terminates when a scalar object is found. Measurements performed on the Rice University Computer showed that 10-15% of total data references were made through codewords.

Arrays can be extended in length by allocating additional storage and modifying the codeword. Multidimensional array addressing is aided by the fact that each codeword can specify an index register. For example, a two-dimensional array can be described by a primary codeword pointing to a table of codewords, one for each row. No address computation is required because the index registers are used to hold the column and row indices. In addition, the rows can be of different lengths.

Although the designers stressed the importance of array addressing and extensibility, perhaps more important is the use of codewords as object names. Using the Rice scheme, a procedure need only specify a codeword parameter to pass an object to another procedure. The codeword completely defines access to the object, including its address and length.

The Rice University Computer had several limitations, but they were often due to implementation decisions. For example, codewords contained the length of the block they defined, but the length was not used by hardware to validate an array index. Instead, a trap facility was provided to allow software to check

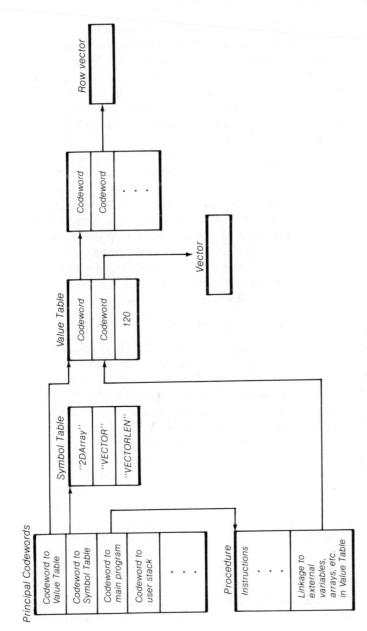

Figure 2-4: Rice University Computer Memory Organization

array bounds. There was also no hardware-enforced memory protection in the system; however, this was due to the simplified goals of the machine. One of the more troublesome shortcomings was that procedure return address links were stored as physical addresses, so procedures could not be relocated easily.

Iliffe and Jodeit suggest that extensions for multiprogramming would be straightforward and require that each user have a separate primary codeword list. Virtual arrays would be possible also, but the only secondary storage on the Rice computer was a magnetic tape system. The Rice implementation of codewords closely resembles the capability concept in the sense that possession of the codeword (or knowledge of its address) is required to access an object. The designers also suggest that Rice codewords could be extended to include usage statistics and that device controllers could be developed to understand codeword formats. These additions were never made, but several architectural advances were made in a follow-on design, the Basic Language Machine.

2.4 The Basic Language Machine

The Basic Language Machine (BLM) [Iliffe 68, Iliffe 69] attempted to extend the capabilities of the Rice University Computer and correct some of its shortcomings. Like the Rice University machine, the BLM incorporated a codeword mechanism, but it added data type tagging and address manipulation as well. An additional goal of the BLM project was to build a machine defined in terms of higher level functions, hiding from the programmer the bit-level details of the machine. The Basic Language (not the familiar BASIC programming language used today) defined this high-level architectural interface in terms of an assembly-level command structure. Design of the BLM was started in 1964, and an experimental version was built by the research division of International Computers Limited (ICL) in the United Kingdom.

The Basic Language Machine supports 8-bit byte, 32-bit word, and 64-bit double-word information units. There are 16 general-purpose registers, each 64 bits long. One of the registers is the program counter (called the *control number*), one points to a data structure containing the context local to the current process (called the *Process Base*), and two are reserved for special escape actions. Memory on the BLM is segmented, the largest segment containing 64K elements of the largest information unit. The BLM supports a 24-bit physical address space.

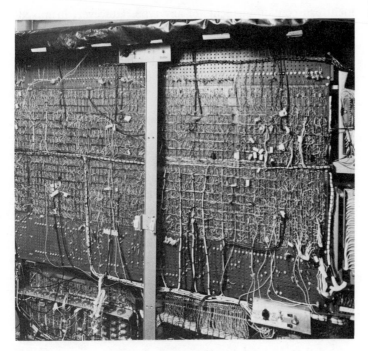

The BLM computer. (Courtesy International Computers Ltd.)

BLM segments are addressed through codewords, as on the Rice computer. However, BLM codewords contain a *type* field indicating the type of information elements stored in the segment they address. The defined data types are:

- 32-bit binary word,
- 8-bit byte,
- 64-bit long numeric,
- 32-bit short numeric,
- mixed type,
- instruction,
- absolute codeword, and
- relative codeword.

The type field also indicates what access is permitted to the segment: data segments can be read-only or read/write; codeword and instruction segments are read-only.

Most of the type encodings specify segments that are homogeneous, that is, segments with only one data type. If the codeword type field specifies a mixed-type segment, the seg-

31

ment can contain elements of any type. However, in mixed-type segments, each element must contain its own tag. A tag is a field contained within the information unit indicating its interpretation. All elements in a mixed-type segment are 64 bits long and contain a 3-bit tag. The four tags defined are:

- 32-bit binary word,
- escape (an attempt to use such an element as an operand causes a trap to software),
- 45-bit address (stored in 64 bits), and
- 61-bit floating numeric element.

The BLM automatically performs conversion and tagging of data elements on fetch or store operations. In homogeneous sets, tags do not need to be stored with each data item, but are constructed from the type stored in the codeword used to load the item into a register. Therefore, homogeneous information can be tightly packed without tagging overhead. The format of 32-bit and 61-bit numeric elements when stored in registers, for example, is shown in Figure 2-5. The tag values of zero and three in the figure indicate 32- and 61-bit numerics, respectively. If an 8-bit byte is fetched, it is automatically sign-extended to 32 bits, and the tag is set to zero.

The BLM is a multiprogrammed computer, and a Process Base defines the execution environment for each process. It is possible for several processes to share the same base and, hence, share access to the same objects. The process address space is composed of a collection of segments, each of which is described by a codeword. The segments may be arranged in a tree structure, but all nodes are reachable only through codewords originating in the Process Base. That is, the terminal nodes of the tree structure contain data or instructions, while the intermediate or branching nodes are codeword sets. Codewords are thus used both to separate user address spaces and to separate logical entities within a program.

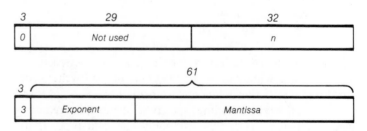

Figure 2-5: Example of BLM Numeric Formats

Relative codewords are provided so that, in situations where it is natural to do so, codewords can be stored in the same segment with the data they describe. To simplify packing, relative codewords are only 32 bits long and can only reference objects within 4096 bytes of their location. Relative codewords allow efficient storage of related data structures. A program can maintain several data structures in a single segment by placing relative codewords for the data structures in the first few segment locations.

Figure 2-6 shows a sample structure of a BLM process. In this case, the Process Base contains codewords for instruction segments, data segments, and codeword segments. The terminal nodes are all data segments. One of the terminal nodes is a mixed segment with relative codewords pointing to internal data structures.

Codewords define the address space and are read-only; they cannot be manipulated by users. BLM *addresses*, however, are quantities derived from codewords that can be user-manipulated. Both addresses and codewords contain the same information, as shown in Figure 2-7: the address and length of the defined set, its type, and a tag indicating an addressing element. Once an address is derived from a codeword, through an operation called *codeword evaluation*, it can be modified through special instructions. MOD and LIM instructions address a subset of the original segment by modifying the loca-

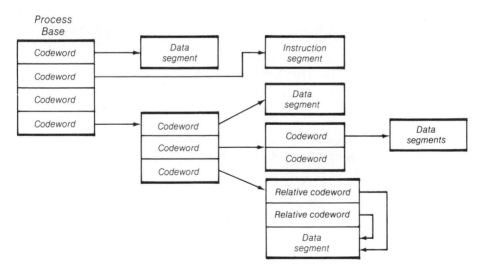

Figure 2-6: Basic Language Machine Addressing

33

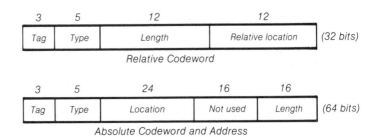

Figure 2-7: BLM Address and Codeword Formats

tion and length fields—to remove a specified number of elements from the beginning or end of the segment, respectively. Looping instructions are available to step addresses through consecutive elements of a segment (performing an implicit MOD by one each time) and to test when the last element has been examined. Iliffe notes that it would be possible also to use the 16 free bits in an absolute codeword to implement linked data structures.

BLM addresses allow users to save intermediate address computations through a tree of codewords. (In contrast, on the Rice University Computer, a full address computation is required on each access to an indirectly referenced object.) On the BLM, the programmer can compute the object address once and save it. The address for a single element in a set can also be computed and saved. Of course, relocation is difficult because addresses as well as codewords must be examined when an object is relocated; that is, BLM addresses are not virtual but contain the primary memory location of a data element.

The Basic Language Machine made several important advances over the Rice University Computer. First, it extended the design to encompass multiprogramming, using a separate Process Base for each process. Second, it provided a more general addressing structure to give users flexibility in performing address arithmetic and saving results. Third, it used a relatively efficient typing mechanism to reduce the number of operators in the instruction set. However, despite the advantages of its structure, the experimental BLM was dismantled in 1970 and no product evolved from the research effort.

2.5 Discussion

The machines described in this section share two major traits: segmentation and the use of descriptors (called code-

words in the Rice and BLM machines) for segment addressing.
Segmentation of programs was used:

- to separate programs into logical entities (procedures and arrays, for example),
- to separate user processes from each other,
- to represent and address complex data structures in hardware, and
- to allow relocation and dynamic growth of data structures.

In general, an address is specified by two parts: a segment descriptor and an offset. However, different approaches for the specifics of addressing and address manipulation were used for each machine. For example, array addressing on the Burroughs B5000 required the index to be pushed onto the stack before the array reference was made. Multidimensional array address calculation required a series of index pushes and evaluations. The Rice University Computer used index registers, and multilevel indexed addressing was performed automatically with an index register specified for each level in the addressing tree. With the BLM, this idea was abandoned and replaced by address modification instructions that allow a controlled form of user-modifiable codewords.

All three machines provide a single base segment that defines a program's execution environment: the B5000 Program Reference Table, the Rice University Computer primary codeword list, and the BLM Process Base. The address of the base segment is usually held in a hardware register. From the base segment, the addressing mechanism provides for the representation of programs and data structures as tree structures. The trees are slightly different in each case due to the differences in addressing. The root of the tree is the base segment hardware register, and the first level nodes are in the Process Base. Starting at the Process Base, the branchpoints of the tree are codewords or descriptors and the leaves are data elements (in the case of the Rice University Computer) or data segments (in the case of B5000 or BLM). The BLM allows a program to traverse several levels and save the intermediate address of a subtree, but the Rice machine requires a complete multilevel scan for each access. The tree structure allows the user to represent complex data structures directly in hardware and to share substructures. Different processes can share subtrees by sharing subtree descriptor segments.

One of the major reasons for segmentation in these systems was to simplify relocation of programs and data. Relocation is facilitated by forcing all references to flow through descriptors. To relocate a segment, the operating system needed only to modify its descriptors. The additional level of indirection provided by descriptors also made segments easily "virtualizable," that is, all segments did not have to occupy primary memory while a program was running. Of course, the complexity of relocation is greatly influenced by the generality with which descriptors can be used. For example, if descriptors are stored in a single descriptor table, relocation involves only a scan of that table. However, if descriptors are stored in segments and each descriptor contains a segment base address, then many segments may need to be searched. Such a memory search can be simplified if segments are typed, as on the BLM, because only mixed or codeword segments would need to be examined.

Care must be taken in any scheme in which multiple copies of the physical segment information can exist for a single segment. This problem could be reduced if the descriptors themselves referred indirectly to a second-level segment descriptor. However, on the machines examined in this chapter, a descriptor contains all of the physical information describing a segment. Thus, copying a descriptor duplicates the physical address.

Descriptors on the B5000 can be copied onto the stack, requiring a possible stack search in order to relocate a segment. However, because it is exclusively a high-level language machine, the use of descriptors can be restricted by the B5000's compilers. The Rice University Computer allows descriptors to exist in any segment of codeword or mixed type, so these segments would need to be scanned. The BLM, on the other hand, allows pure codeword segments and relative codewords within other word-oriented segments. Both the Rice and BLM machines require a tree search to find descriptors for segments to be relocated.

Another problem in multiprogramming systems is controlling access to shared segments. A user (or I/O device) wishing to perform a multistep transaction on a shared segment must gain exclusive access to that segment. This can be achieved by disabling interrupts or context switching (usually via executive procedures), through the use of explicit software locks, or through the use of a "lockout" or software trap bit in the descriptor. If lockout bits are used, then the executive must find all copies of descriptors for the target segment.

Another issue in descriptor design is the cost of indirection.

All of the examined machines allow tree-structured data. Although the Rice machine has automatic multilevel addressing, the Burroughs and the BLM require several manual steps. However, the Burroughs and the BLM allow for partial address computations to be saved.

One of the perpetual debates in computer architecture is the tradeoff between the use of tag bits in data elements and the larger operation code set needed in non-tagged architectures. The BLM scheme seems to answer the concern for tagging overhead by only storing tags in the codeword or address for homogeneous segments. However, for mixed or heterogeneous structures, each element must still carry a tag. In addition, the elements in a mixed set must all be of the same size as the largest element in the set; that is, all elements must have the same alignment to protect against addressing the middle of some element and interpreting data bits as tags. This is not particularly efficient because any segment containing a codeword pointer must use 64 bits for each element. Still, there are benefits to tagging besides the possible savings of operation code bits, including automatic conversion and checking by the hardware. A certain amount of error detection may also be gained by self-tagging of information units.

A likely problem with these machines was that of garbage collection. If a program can write a descriptor to a descriptor segment, the descriptor previously occupying that memory word could be overwritten. If the overwritten descriptor were the only one referencing some segment, that segment would then be unreachable. In general, this problem was prevented by making descriptor segments read-only. The B5000 PRT was not read-only; however, this system relied heavily on the compilers for proper system operation. User programs did not have direct control of the PRT or descriptors. Garbage segments were considered a problem on the BLM, and a garbage collection process was written to search for unreachable segments.

One of the more important gains from the use of descriptors is the protection of procedures. If procedures can be invoked only by referencing a descriptor, then two benefits are realized. First, a procedure can only be invoked at its entry point contained in the descriptor; it cannot be entered at a random point. Second, procedure code is protected from accidental or deliberate modification.

Despite their differences, all of these machines have a common link to capability architectures: they all use descriptors to name programming objects. The objects are generally simple, for example, a segment containing an array, a procedure, or a list. I/O operations are also described by descriptors on the B5000.

It is important to note that all of these machines support large word lengths. A single word is large enough to contain all of the segment base and limit information as well as various other bits. In general, although bytes may be supported as data types, byte addressing is not provided; that is, memory is word-addressable. The descriptor is a single word that contains all of the physical information needed to locate the object in primary or secondary memory. In retrospect, this fact is important because duplicating the descriptor duplicates all of the segment mapping information. Descriptors are therefore different from virtual addresses or modern capabilities where a second level of addressing is employed.

Although the Rice family of machines was not directly continued, the B5000 led to many stack and descriptor machines in the Burroughs family, and other manufacturers were also influenced by its design. Whether or not they were long-lived, these machines demonstrated the feasibility of using descriptors and segmentation to greatly increase programming flexibility for the user, the compilers, and the operating system.

2.6 For Further Reading

The Burroughs B5000 is described in *The Descriptor* [Burroughs 61], a remarkably modern document for the time it was written. One section of the manual is devoted to the advantages of high-level language systems (ALGOL in this case), such as reduced programming time, simplified debugging, and program maintenance. Such goals are remarkably similar to the objectives of today's object-based systems.

Two papers that discuss storage allocation in the Rice University Computer are [Iliffe 62] and [Jodeit 68]. A book is available on the Basic Language Machine [Iliffe 68]; however, it is unfortunate that more was not published on the machine's design and use. Perhaps this indicates the fate of industry's research projects that never become products. However, an excellent discussion of the BLM within the context of modern capability systems appears in [Iliffe 82].

Following the BLM, design of a third member of the Rice

computer family, called the Rice Research Computer, was
started at Rice University [Feustel 72]. The Rice Research
Computer was to be a high-performance tagged architecture,
but technological problems caused the termination of the project in 1974. A discussion of the general advantages of tagged
architectures can be found in [Feustel 73].

Early Capability Architectures

3.1 Introduction

Although the Burroughs, Rice, and BLM systems included capability-like addressing structures, the word "capability" was not introduced until 1966, by Dennis and Van Horn of MIT [Dennis 66]. Dennis and Van Horn defined a hypothetical operating system supervisor for a multiprogramming system. Multiprogramming systems were already in use at that time; however, many difficult problems had yet to be solved. The MIT design used the concept of capability addressing to provide a uniform solution to several issues in multiprogramming systems, including sharing and cooperation between processes, protection of processes, debugging, and naming of objects.

The concept of capability addressing presented by Dennis and Van Horn quickly found its way into several hardware and software systems. This chapter first describes the Dennis and Van Horn supervisor and its use of capabilities and then examines some of the early systems influenced by its design.

3.2 Dennis and Van Horn's Supervisor

Dennis and Van Horn's operating system supervisor is defined by a set of objects and a set of operations for each type of object. The operations, implemented by the supervisor, are called *meta-instructions*. To describe this system and its meta-instructions involves the introduction of the following terms:

- *segment*—an addressable collection of consecutive memory words,
- *process*—a thread of control through an instruction stream, and
- *computation*—one or more processes that share an addressing environment and cooperate to solve a task.

A process is the basic execution entity. A process executes within an environment called a *sphere of protection* or *domain*. The sphere of protection for a process defines the segments that it can address, the I/O operations that it can perform, and other objects, such as directories, that it can manipulate.

As part of its state, a process in the Dennis and Van Horn system contains a pointer to a list of *capabilities*, called a *C-list* for short. Each capability in the C-list names an object in the system and specifies the access rights permitted to that object. The name is a pointer that the supervisor can use to locate the object; however, the authors suggest that systems avoid the use of physical attributes such as addresses for pointers. The name is a unique bit string assigned to an object when it is created. The naming of objects in an address-independent manner simplifies relocation and management of memory.

The access rights in a capability are specific to the type of object named. For example, the rights bits allow execute, read, read/execute, read/write, or read/write/execute access for segments. Each capability also contains a single bit indicating whether or not its possessor is the owner of the object. An object's owner has special rights with respect to the object, such as the ability to delete it.

Each process in the system, then, has a pointer to a single C-list containing capabilities naming all of the objects it can access. When executing a supervisor meta-instruction, the process specifies capabilities by their index in the C-list. A computation consists of several potentially cooperating processes that share a single sphere of protection. That is, the processes in a computation share the same C-list. Figure 3-1 shows three processes that make up two distinct computations.

The supervisor allows the creation of tree-structured processes. Using a FORK operation, a process can create a parallel process executing within its sphere of protection. In addition, a process can create and control subprocesses, called *inferior spheres*, that execute in separate subordinate domains. To create an inferior sphere, a process executes a CREATE SPHERE meta-instruction. As a parameter to the meta-instruction, the

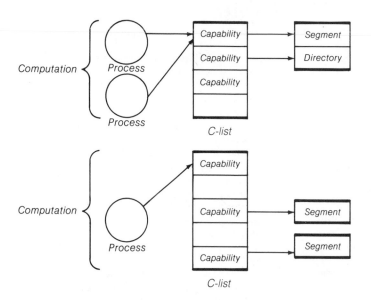

Figure 3-1: Processes, Computations, and C-Lists

process specifies an entry in its C-list, in which the supervisor places a capability for the inferior. This capability can then be used to control the inferior process.

When a process executes a CREATE SPHERE meta-instruction, the supervisor creates the inferior with an empty C-list. Using its capability for the inferior, the parent process can execute meta-instructions to:

- move capabilities from its C-list to the inferior's C-list,
- start and stop the inferior,
- examine or change the inferior's state, and
- remove capabilities from the inferior's C-list.

The creating process can construct any sphere of protection desired for the inferior, with the restriction that the superior's C-list must contain any capabilities to be copied to the inferior's C-list. Table 3-1 lists the Dennis and Van Horn meta-instructions that operate on inferior spheres, capabilities, and directories (which are described in Section 3.6).

Inferior spheres are useful for debugging. When testing a new procedure, a user might like to constrain the environment in which the procedure can execute so that an error will not accidentally destroy the user's objects. When a process creates an inferior sphere, it specifies the address of a procedure to handle any special conditions. If an error or exception is de-

43

CREATE SPHERE	create an inferior sphere and return a process capability to the creator
GRANT	copy a capability to an inferior's C-list with specified access rights
EXAMINE	copy inferior's capability into superior's C-list
UNGRANT	delete capability from inferior's C-list
ENTER	call protected procedure with one capability parameter
RELEASE	remove capability from C-list
CREATE	create a new segment, entry, or directory
PLACE	insert capability and text name into directory
ACQUIRE	search directory for text name and copy associated capability into C-list
REMOVE	remove named item and associated capability from directory
DELETE	delete object specified by name
LINK	obtain capability for another user's root directory and insert in C-list

Table 3-1: Dennis and Van Horn Supervisor Capability Operations

tected in the inferior, the supervisor creates a new process within the sphere of the parent process to execute the error-handling procedure. Or, the inferior can explicitly signal the parent through special meta-instructions. This feature allows a superior to build a supervisory environment for its inferior which is equivalent to that provided by the superior's parent (or by the supervisor).

Although C-lists provide for object addressing, they do not satisfy the need for object naming. Users in a multiprogramming system must be able to identify objects (particularly long-term objects such as files) using mnemonic character string names. They must also be able to share objects with other users in the system. In order to allow users to name objects and retain them indefinitely, the supervisor provides primitives for the creation and manipulation of capability *directories*.

A directory contains a list of directory entries. Each entry consists of a text name, an associated capability, and a single bit specifying whether the entry is private or free. The private/free bit allows a user to share a directory without permitting access to all of the directory entries. Directory entries are accessed by text name, and meta-instructions are provided to copy a directory capability to the user's C-list, place a C-list capability in a directory along with an associated name, or remove a directory entry. The directory meta-instructions—PLACE, ACQUIRE, REMOVE, DELETE, and LINK—are listed among the capability operations in Table 3-1.

Each user has a single root directory that contains capabilities for the user's permanent objects. When a user initiates a session (that is, when the user logs into the system), the supervisor creates a new process and places a capability for the root directory in the process's C-list, giving the process access to these objects. A process can then load capabilities from the root directory into the C-list by executing an ACQUIRE meta-instruction. The ACQUIRE specifies three parameters: the capability for the root directory, the text name of the object to be loaded, and the C-list location in which to place the associated capability.

New directories can be created and capabilities for directories can be stored in other directories. Thus, a user can build graph-structured directory mechanisms and share directories or subdirectories. To facilitate object sharing, the supervisor allows a process to obtain a capability for another process's root directory. In turn, the root directory can be traversed to locate subdirectories, and so on. However, when examining another user's directory structure, only those entries marked as free can be accessed.

The Dennis and Van Horn supervisor does not support a separate concept of files. Any segment or directory is potentially long-lived and can be used to store information from session to session or over system restarts. An object is maintained by the system as long as a capability exists for that object. Therefore, to make a segment or directory long-lived, a user simply stores a capability for that object in the root directory or any long-lived directory reachable through the root. The supervisor automatically deletes an object when the last capability for that object is deleted. Deleting any single capability for an object does not necessarily cause the object to be deleted because other capabilities for the object may still exist. The supervisor does support an explicit DELETE meta-instruction that can be used by a process with owner privileges to an object.

One of the most important aspects of the Dennis and Van Horn supervisor is its support for protected procedures. Within a multiprogramming system, it should be possible for a user to create a procedure that provides service to many different users. However, this procedure must be able to protect local objects from its callers, and the callers may wish to guarantee that the procedure does not destroy or compromise any of their local objects. The protected procedure meets both of these needs.

A process creates a protected procedure by obtaining an *entry capability* through a supervisor meta-instruction. The entry capability contains a pointer to the C-list of the process that created it. It also contains an index, i, and a range, n, for a set of sequential procedure capabilities within the C-list of the creating process. The entry capability can then be passed to any process (through the directory mechanism, for example) and used to call any of the n procedures. To call a protected procedure, a process executes an ENTER meta-instruction specifying:

- an entry capability,
- the index of one of the n procedures to be called, and
- a capability parameter to be passed to the protected procedure.

The entry capability and capability parameter must be in the caller's C-list. As a result of the ENTER instruction, the supervisor creates a new process to execute the protected procedure. This new process executes in the sphere of protection *specified by the C-list pointer contained in the entry capability.* Figure 3-2 shows this change from the sphere of the caller to the sphere of the protected procedure. The entry capability in Figure 3-2 allows its owner to call one of two procedures defined by capabilities in the protected C-list.

A protected procedure, then, executes in the domain de-

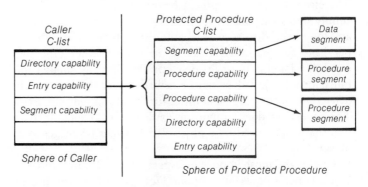

Figure 3-2: Protected Procedure Protection Spheres

fined by the procedure's creator, not in the domain of the caller. In this way, the caller and the protected procedure are mutually isolated. The caller has no access to the protected procedure's objects, and the procedure has no access to the caller's objects, with the exception of those objects passed explicitly through the capability parameter. Because this parameter can be a directory capability as well as a segment capability, a caller can pass a list of capabilities or an arbitrary data structure. A process possessing an entry capability can only use that capability to call one of a sequence of procedures. Once that procedure begins execution, it has access to all of the objects available in its private C-list.

The Dennis and Van Horn conceptual design became very influential on later systems. However, there are many ways to apply the concepts and many problems inherent in doing so. The first system to incorporate the concept of capability was a timesharing system at MIT, which is examined in the following section.

3.3 The MIT PDP-1 Timesharing System

The first computer system to include Dennis and Van Horn's capability operations was a timeshared operating system constructed at MIT from Dennis' design [Ackerman 67, MIT 71]. The system ran on a modified 12K-word Digital Equipment Corporation PDP-1 computer, the first minicomputer. The timesharing system supported five "typewriters" and used capabilities only to reference a few relatively high-level system resources, such as terminals, tapes, and drums. However, the operating system allowed users to extend this set of resources by creating new protected subsystems. It is the protected subsystem mechanism that is briefly examined here.

Each process running on the PDP-1 timesharing system has a C-list (also called the program reference list, after the Burroughs B5000), in which capabilities are held. The C-list is actually maintained in locations 0-77 of process address space. These locations are protected against program examination or modification and can only be manipulated by the operating system. Each capability is addressed by its index in the list.

Capabilities are created by special supervisor instructions. Each capability represents a resource object owned by the process. The supervisor supports a small number of resource types: I/O device, inferior process, file, directory, queue, and entry. When the process wishes to perform an operation on a

resource object, it *invokes* the object's capability through an
INVOKE instruction. The INVOKE instruction specifies: (1) the
C-list index of the capability to be invoked and (2) an operation
to perform on the object represented by the capability. The
INVOKE is similar to the ENTER instruction in the Dennis and
Van Horn design.

Dennis and Van Horn's supervisor allows a process to create
protected procedures that execute in private spheres of protection to protect local data from access by their callers. The
PDP-1 system goes a step further. It allows creation of controlled subsystems that maintain different protected data objects on behalf of different processes, just as the operating system maintains files, for example, on behalf of different
processes. To do this, the subsystem must be able to verify that
a process is permitted access to an invoked object.

A subsystem is accessed through entry capabilities in the
same way that protected procedures are accessed in the Dennis
and Van Horn supervisor. To identify different subsystem resource objects, however, the PDP-1 system allows a subsystem
to create different versions of its entry capabilities. The entry
capabilities for a given subsystem are equivalent except for a
transmitted word field that can be specified by the subsystem
when the entry is created. In this way, the subsystem can
maintain protected data structures on behalf of many processes. When a process calls the subsystem to create a new resource, the subsystem returns an entry capability with a transmitted word uniquely identifying that resource. Subsequently,
when the user invokes an operation on that resource through
the entry capability, the subsystem interrogates the transmitted word to determine which data structures to access. The
transmitted word field is 6 bits in size, allowing a subsystem to
support only 64 different objects; however, the PDP-1 supports a small user community.

The system was in operation for student use until the mid-
1970s. It was distinguished not only by its capability supervisor but also by its space war game that ran on the PDP-1 video
display. Following the MIT PDP-1 system, a major step in
capability systems design took place at the University of Chicago. This work was significant because it used capabilities as a
hardware protection mechanism.

3.4 The Chicago Magic Number Machine

In 1967 a group at the University of Chicago Institute for
Computer Research began work on the Multicomputer, later

called the Chicago Magic Number Machine [Fabry 67, Shepherd 68, Yngve 68]. The goals of the project were ambitious: to provide a general-purpose computing resource for the Institute, to allow computer science research, and to interface to new peripheral devices. The project was perhaps too ambitious; in fact, the system was never completed. Nevertheless, the Chicago effort was the first attempt to build an integrated hardware/software capability system [Fabry 68]. The implementation of capability-based primary memory protection in this machine was to serve as a model for several early capability designs.

The Chicago machine provides a general register architecture and a segmented memory space. Memory is addressed through capabilities, and a process must possess a capability for any segment it addresses. Capabilities can be stored in registers or in memory; however, they cannot be mixed with data. Therefore, the machine supports two sets of registers—*data registers* and *capability registers*, and two types of segments—*data segments* and *capability segments*.

There are sixteen 16-bit, general-purpose data registers, three of which can be used as index registers. Capabilities are stored in six capability registers, each holding multiple 16-bit fields because capabilities are longer than the machine's 16-bit words. Several bits in each segment capability indicate whether the addressed segment contains data or capabilities. Hardware LOAD and STORE instructions allow programs to move capabilities between capability registers and capability segments, but programs are prohibited from performing data operations on capabilities. A process can have many capability segments, and capabilities can be copied freely between them.

For a program to access an element in a memory segment, the program must first load a capability for that segment into a capability register. The capability registers therefore act as a hardware C-list. A capability for a memory segment describes:

- the segment base *address*,
- the segment *length*,
- the *type* of the segment (data or capability),
- an *activity code*, indicating whether the segment is in primary memory or secondary store, and
- an *access code*, indicating how the segment may be used.

The access codes for data segments are read, read/execute, read/write, and read/write/execute; the access codes for capability segments are enter, enter/read, and enter/read/write. A program with capability read and capability write access to a capability segment can execute capability load and store operations on that segment, but cannot perform data operations on the capabilities. A user is never given data access to a capability segment, because that would allow the user to fabricate capabilities. However, the operating system supervisor may keep capabilities permitting data access to a user's capability segments. The supervisor uses these capabilities to perform meta-instructions that create a new capability or modify a capability.

To access an operand in primary memory, an instruction specifies a memory address using three components:

- a capability register containing a segment capability,
- a data register or literal value specifying the relative offset of a data element in the segment, and
- an optional index register containing an index that can be added to the supplied offset.

This allows, for example, addressing of an array that is located within a data segment. The hardware computes the sum of the two offsets and the base address contained in the capability to generate the primary memory address. It also verifies that the address lies within the segment, that the type of access is legal, and that the segment is in primary memory.

Segments can be created, extended, and destroyed by execution of supervisor meta-instructions, as shown in Table 3-2. A meta-instruction is also available to copy (snapshot) a segment onto secondary storage. The snapshot operation requires as a parameter the number of days the copy should be maintained. The current state of a segment and all backup copies are identified by the same capability, but the backups are differentiated by the time and date the copy was made. When a program retrieves a snapshot, the supervisor allocates a memory segment, copies the snapshot to that segment, and returns a new capability for that new segment to the user.

The Magic Number Machine is a multiprogramming system in which each process has as part of its state:

- a name,
- a capability for an account to be charged for its resource usage,

CREATE SEGMENT	create a new segment of given size and type and return a capability for it
CHANGE SEGMENT SIZE	
	increase or decrease segment size
DESTROY SEGMENT	delete segment
SNAPSHOT	copy current segment state to backing storage, marked with current time and date
RETRIEVE	copy specified snapshot from backing store into a new segment
CHANGE ACCESS CODE	
	produce a new version of a capability with reduced access rights
EXAMINE CAPABILITY	
	several meta-instructions to allow inspection of segment size, type, ID, access code, and activity code
CREATE PROCESS	create a subordinate process and return a process capability
MAIL	send capability and associated text name to specified user

Table 3-2:   Chicago Magic Number Supervisor Capability Operations

- a capability for a base capability segment addressing the user's objects, and
- a capability for a mailbox.

Interprocess communication takes place between process mailboxes. A mailbox consists of a capability segment and an associated data segment. Using the MAIL meta-instruction, a process can send a capability and an associated informational text name to another process that can read, copy, or delete the information.

In addition to the hardware registers and the information listed above, each process has two segments associated with its context: a *process data segment* and *process capability segment*. Each of these segments has a fixed-sized storage region followed by a stack for data or capabilities. Two capability registers are reserved to address these segments, and two data registers act as stack pointers, although there are no explicit stack instructions (i.e., the registers must be manually updated).

A protected procedure mechanism in the Chicago Magic Number Machine allows for efficient one-way protection; that is, the procedure is protected from its caller but the caller is not protected from the procedure. Each protected procedure consists of at least one program segment and one capability segment, called the *linkage segment*, as shown in Figure 3-3. An

51

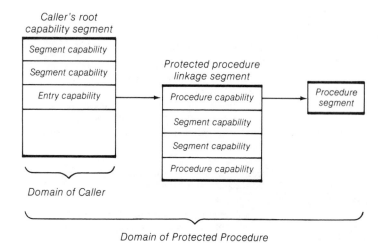

Figure 3-3: Chicago Magic Number Machine Linkage Segment

entry capability for the procedure points to the linkage segment, which contains capabilities for all objects needed by the procedure such as instruction segments, data segments, I/O operations, and so on. The first capability in the linkage segment points to the procedure entry point. Possession of an enter-only capability for the linkage segment allows the possessor to call the procedure using this first capability, but permits no other linkage segment access. Thus, the protected procedure can execute in a richer environment than its caller because it can access the entire linkage segment. Parameters can be passed either on the stack or in the registers.

Work on the Chicago Multicomputer/Magic Number Machine was eventually abandoned due to lack of funding. Although the project was never completed, the design was passed on to others including a group at Berkeley who incorporated some of its features into a new operating system, which is described next.

3.5 The CAL-TSS System

Started in the summer of 1968 at the University of California at Berkeley's computer center, the CAL-TSS project was an attempt to implement a general-purpose, capability-based operating system on conventional hardware. CAL-TSS was designed to supply timesharing services to several hundred users of a CDC 6400 computer system, thereby replacing

CDC's SCOPE operating system. Work on design and implementation continued until the fall of 1971, when it became clear that the system could not meet its goals in terms of service and performance. Funding was stopped and the project abandoned. Since then, its designers have published several appraisals of the project's successes and failures [Sturgis 74, Lampson 76].

The CAL-TSS operating system is a layered design in which each layer provides a virtual machine to the next higher layer. Each layer is specified as a set of objects and operations on those objects. This section examines the innermost layer of the supervisor which handles capabilities and object addressing.

The basic unit of protection in the CAL-TSS system is a *domain*, an environment containing hardware registers, primary memory, and a C-list. (A domain corresponds to the sphere of protection in the Dennis and Van Horn supervisor.) Access to objects outside the domain can occur only through *invocation* of a C-list capability; the possessor of a capability *invokes* an operation on the object it addresses by specifying the capability, the operation to be performed, and other optional parameters. A *process* is the execution entity of a domain, and its C-list may contain capabilities for other subordinate processes over which it exercises control.

Capabilities in the CAL-TSS system have three components:

- a *type* field that specifies the nature of the object addressed,
- an *option bits* field that indicates operations which can be performed by the possessor of the capability, and
- a *value* field that identifies the object and contains a pointer to the object.

Each capability occupies two 60-bit words in a C-list. A process has a root C-list and can create new second-level C-lists. When a process invokes a supervisor operation, it can specify capabilities stored in either the root C-list or any second-level C-list as parameters. A capability specification can therefore consist of two indices: one to locate a C-list capability in the root C-list and another for the target capability in a second-level C-list.

The CAL-TSS supervisor implements eight types of objects. A process can call supervisor operations to create and manipulate the following object types:

- kernel files (simple sequential byte streams),
- C-lists,

- event channels (interprocess communication channels),
- processes,
- allocation blocks (for accounting and resource control),
- labels (for naming short-lived objects and domains),
- capability-creating authorizations (user subsystems), and
- operations.

The last two supervisor-implemented types listed, capability-creating authorizations and operations, will be discussed later.

One important advance of CAL-TSS over its predecessors is in its physical object addressing. When the CAL-TSS supervisor creates a new object, it assigns that object a unique identifier. The identifier for that object is never reused, even after the object is destroyed. The use of unique identifiers solves a difficult system problem. If, for example, an object identifier could be reused after object deletion, the supervisor would have to guarantee that all capabilities for an object are destroyed before the object is destroyed. Otherwise, the remaining capabilities would be *dangling references*, that is, pointers to an object that does not exist. Were the supervisor to reuse the identifier later for a newly created object, such dangling references could be used inadvertently to modify the new object.

The CAL-TSS kernel provides a second level of indirection in addressing to greatly simplify relocation. Primary memory addressing of objects occurs through a single system table: the Master Object Table (MOT). The MOT is a kernel data structure that contains entries for every object in the system. Each MOT entry holds the unique object identifier and the primary memory address of one object's data. CAL-TSS capabilities do not contain primary memory addresses. Instead, a capability contains the unique identifier for the object it addresses and an index into the Master Object Table.

Figure 3-4 illustrates a C-list capability and the Master Object Table. The capability addresses a file object, as indicated by the type field shown symbolically as *"File."* The capability's value field contains the index of the MOT entry, M, which in turn contains the primary memory address of the file. All capabilities for the same file will contain the same MOT index. If the supervisor needs to relocate the file's primary memory segment, only a single MOT entry will have to be changed.

Both the capability and the MOT entry shown in Figure 3-4 contain the file object's unique identifier, IDx. The supervisor verifies that the identifiers in the capability and the MOT entry

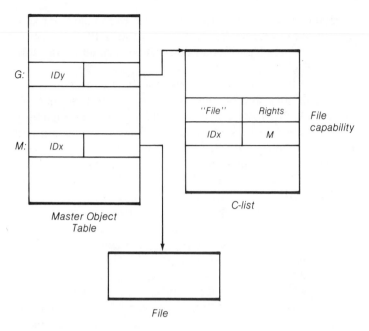

Figure 3-4: CAL-TSS Object Addressing

are identical for every operation invoked on the capability.
When an object is deleted, the supervisor increments the identifier field of the object's MOT entry. Any subsequent attempt
to use a capability for the deleted object (a dangling reference)
would fail because the identifiers would not match.

Note that the C-list in Figure 3-4 is also a supervisor object
and is addressed by the MOT entry at index G. The unique
identifier for the C-list is IDy, an identifier that would be
stored in any capabilities addressing the C-list.

The CAL-TSS system supports two object types that allow
users to extend the small set of supervisor-implemented objects. A *capability-creating authorization* is an object permitting
its possessor to create private capabilities for a private user-
defined subsystem. Each user subsystem implements a single
new type. To use this facility, a subsystem executes a supervisor meta-instruction to receive a capability for a capability-
creating authorization object. The authorization object contains a new system-wide, *unique* type field. The subsystem can
then present this capability to the supervisor, along with a 60-
bit value, and obtain a new capability containing the subsystem's type and the specified value. The value inserted in the

55

capability corresponds to the transmitted word field that a sub-system can insert into capabilities on the MIT PDP-1 supervisor; it uniquely identifies an object implemented by the subsystem.

Such private capabilities receive the same protection as system capabilities, and can only be stored in C-lists and manipulated by kernel meta-instructions. Thus, a private capability can be passed to another domain to indicate ownership and rights to an object protected by the subsystem. For example, a user could implement a protected mail subsystem with the operations CREATE MAILBOX, DESTROY MAILBOX, READ MAIL, and WRITE MAIL. The subsystem would first obtain a capability-creating authorization containing a unique type field. Another domain calling the create mailbox operation would receive a capability containing the mailbox subsystem's type field and a unique value field to identify the newly created mailbox. The possessor of the capability could later present it to the mail system in order to read, write, or delete that mailbox, but could not modify the capability or directly access the mailbox representation. In this way, users can build subsystems that extend facilities provided by the base operating system.

A CAL-TSS *operation* is a supervisor-implemented object that allows the possessor to request a kernel or private meta-instruction; that is, to invoke a service. The operation object is a list describing the service to be performed, followed by specification of how the parameters are to be obtained. If the operation is for a private domain, that domain must be named along with an indication of the service requested. The parameter list specifies whether each parameter is: (1) data in the caller's memory, (2) a capability in the caller's C-list, (3) immediate data in the operation list itself, or (4) a fixed capability stored in the operation list.

The ability to contain immediate capabilities in the parameter list of an operation object is a powerful feature. It allows the called domain to receive a capability not available to the caller and thus is similar to the Chicago machine linkage segment. However, because the designers did not realize this advantage of operation objects until sometime after the system was constructed, the feature was never used.

When the CAL-TSS project was finally terminated in 1971, it had become clear that the system would never live up to expectations for either performance or functionality. There were many reasons for this, some being crucial design flaws.

One of the major design difficulties was the hardware base: a CDC 6400 with 32K 60-bit words of primary memory and 300K words of extended core storage (ECS). ECS is a memory device used as high-speed secondary storage. It is not used for execution, but data can be block-transferred between ECS and main storage at rates of several megawords per second. Management of ECS was one of the principal design problems. Equally troublesome was the 6400 memory management support, consisting of only a single base and limit register pair. Nevertheless, much was learned from the CAL-TSS project about the design choices available to capability system implementors.

3.6 Discussion

This chapter has examined early attempts to define and implement capability-based hardware and software systems. All of the systems described were designed in the late 1960s. These systems show one obvious relationship to the machines examined in the previous chapter: capabilities are descriptors used to address memory segments and other system objects. In a sense, the difference is merely one of terminology. The concept of capabilities and the C-list, as Dennis and Van Horn state, follows from the B5000's descriptors and Program Reference Table. However, there are some significant conceptual differences in the general way capability addressing is applied, in the lifetimes of capabilities and the objects addressed, and in the protected procedure mechanism that allows users to extend the functions of the operating system supervisor.

Capabilities are protected addresses; that is, a process can create new capabilities in its C-list only by calling a supervisor meta-instruction. Once a process receives a capability, it cannot directly modify the bits in the capability. The capabilities accessible to a process at any time define its sphere of protection or domain. All of the addresses (that is, capabilities) which a process can specify must either be contained in its domain at the time the process is created or be obtained through interaction with the kernel or other domains.

Because capabilities must be protected from user modification, these systems chose to isolate them within C-lists. C-lists are implemented as one or more segments that user processes cannot directly write with data instructions. Capabilities cannot be embedded in user data. This requirement is somewhat restrictive because complex data structures that include pointers cannot always be naturally represented. The problem often can be circumvented by storing a C-list index in the data rather than the capability itself. However, storing a C-list index in place of a capability makes sharing data structures difficult if the processes do not share the same C-list. Another problem caused by the segregation of capabilities and data is the need for separate stacks and registers. Machines that support capabilities must have both data and capability stacks and data and capability registers. An alternative would be to support tagging, as in the BLM.

While the Dennis and Van Horn supervisor allows each process to have only one C-list, users of the Chicago Magic Number Machine and the CAL-TSS can store capabilities in multiple capability segments, chaining them together as desired to form complex tree or graph structures. The ability to construct additional C-lists allows fine-grained sharing of capabilities. Small C-lists can be created for sharing small collections of objects. The C-list addressing mechanism has a significant affect on the sharing of capabilities and the protection of objects. For example, if a procedure addresses its objects by C-list index, the procedure cannot be shared unless the sharing processes store the procedure's objects in the same locations in their respective C-lists. However, if a procedure executes with its own C-list, in which it places capabilities passed as parameters by its callers, this problem does not arise.

To compensate for the single C-list, Dennis and Van Horn allow capability directories for storage of capabilities and associated text names. The capability directory concept is a powerful extension of the directories provided by most operating systems. Even on most contemporary computers, directories can only be used to name files. In contrast, a capability directory allows the user to name and store many different object types. Directories can be shared between domains, and the Dennis and Van Horn system allows any user to obtain a capability for another user's root directory. A user can protect directory entries from external examination by setting a private bit associated with each entry. However, this mechanism in itself is insufficient for selective sharing among several users, because it is impossible to grant privileges to one user that are denied to another.

An additional method for exchanging capabilities between domains is the mail facility of the Chicago machine. Each domain has a local mailbox consisting of a capability and data segment pair used to receive capabilities and symbolic capability names. Mailing a capability is equivalent to transferring a single directory entry between domains. It is unclear whether any additional information is placed in the mailbox, but some authentication information for the sender, either with the message or added by the mail system, probably should be required.

All of the systems examined support subordinate processes and process tree structures. A superior process is given complete control of an inferior that it creates. The superior defines the domain of the inferior by granting capabilities. It has the power to start, stop, modify the state of, generate simulated interrupts to, and service faults for the inferior. Mechanisms such as this allow users to build and test complex subsystems and to debug inferior processes. It may also be possible to simulate the kernel or hardware environment and, depending on the completeness of the mechanism, to debug kernel procedures.

Protected procedure mechanisms are available on all of these early systems. Dennis and Van Horn provide protected procedures through entry capabilities. The creator of the protected procedure obtains an entry and makes it public for users of the service. The protected procedure executes in a separate process in its creator's domain and receives a single capability parameter from its caller. The caller and callee are isolated from each other. In the CAL-TSS system, protected procedures also execute in a separate domain, with an operation object serving as the entry. The operation object specifies some number of data and/or capability parameters and methods to obtain them. The Chicago machine sacrifices two-way isolation for the improved performance of a one-way mechanism. A protected procedure on the Chicago machine executes in the domain of its caller and has access to its caller's objects. The protected procedure also has access to private capabilities contained in its linkage segment. Parameters are passed on the stack or in registers.

In addition to protected procedures, the MIT PDP-1 and CAL-TSS systems allow user processes to manufacture private capabilities. This type-extension mechanism allows user programs to extend kernel facilities in a uniform manner by creating new object types. User-created operations are invoked in the same way that supervisor meta-instructions are invoked.

The CAL-TSS capability-creating authorization and the MIT PDP-1 transmitted word facilities are *sealing* mechanisms. A value is sealed in the capability that is not directly usable by the possessor of that capability. When passed back to the implementing subsystem, the subsystem—using a special capability it maintains—can *unseal* the value to determine which object the capability addresses. Sealing mechanisms are also provided by the Chicago machine's linkage segments and by CAL-TSS operations. In these systems, capabilities are sealed inside of special linkage segments. An entry capability for the linkage segment only allows its possessor to call procedures through specific entries in the segment. As a result of the CALL or ENTER instruction, the linkage segment is unsealed and its capabilities made available to the called procedure.

Perhaps the most important generalization of addressing provided by capabilities is support for long-lived objects. Capabilities allow uniform addressing of both short-term and long-term objects. Traditional computer systems require different addressing mechanisms for primary memory, secondary memory files, and supervisor-implemented objects. A capability can be used to address abstract objects of any type and any lifetime, implemented by either hardware or software. This advantage of capability systems raises a number of issues: how large must capabilities be to address the longer lifetime of objects, how can capabilities and objects be saved on secondary storage, what happens if capabilities or objects are deleted, how does the system know when an object can be deleted, and so on?

The Dennis and Van Horn supervisor allows objects to live an arbitrary length of time. An object exists until it is explicitly deleted or until all capabilities pointing to the object are removed. Thus, all objects are potentially long-lived, and the system must be capable of determining when the last capability for an object is deleted, or secondary storage will eventually become filled with garbage objects. Directories are used to keep track of long-term objects and their capabilities and to allow user reference to these objects by symbolic names. In the Chicago Magic Number Machine, snapshots are made of objects to force them to secondary storage. The objects can be retrieved later, although the issue of storing capabilities was not addressed by the design. When an object is retrieved from disk in the Chicago system, it is not retrieved as the same object but is placed in a new segment for which a new capability is generated.

One of the critical shortcomings of the CAL-TSS system was its failure to provide uniform addressing for permanent storage. The CAL-TSS system differentiated between user objects, which could be saved on secondary storage, and kernel objects, which could not be saved on secondary storage. Moreover, because user objects were stored merely as byte streams, the CAL-TSS system could not save C-lists on disk while maintaining protection system integrity. The decision to support different object lifetimes, based on the belief that kernel objects were short-lived and would not require permanent storage, led to many quirks in the operating system.

Finally, one of the most important features in these systems was the physical implementation of addressing. Like earlier descriptor systems, the Chicago Magic Number Machine maintained hardware location information in the capability itself. This led to the relocation problems of descriptor systems; that is, relocation of a segment required a search for all capabilities addressing that segment. CAL-TSS took an important step by separating the capability from the addressing information, as recommended by Dennis and Van Horn. The physical relocation information is held in a central Master Object Table, and the capability contains a MOT index and a unique object identifier. Thus, relocation does not require a search for an object's capabilities. Deletion of an object also requires no search, because an attempt to use the capability for a deleted object will fail when the kernel checks the unique identifier in the MOT entry.

The Dennis and Van Horn supervisor defined the formal concepts of capability addressing. The MIT PDP-1 system, the Chicago Magic Number Machine, and the CAL-TSS system were the first trial implementations. The MIT timesharing system was in operation for several years, providing service to a small number of users, although capabilities were not a central part of the system's design. The Chicago and CAL-TSS systems were much more ambitious in terms of design, implementation, and goals. Perhaps the problem with these systems was the expectation that they would provide service to a large user community. In this sense, both systems failed, because neither was completed. However, when viewed as research projects, these early systems explored the crucial design issues and demonstrated both the advantages and difficulties of using an important new addressing technique.

3.7 For Further Reading

Dennis and Van Horn's publication paved the way for research in capability- and object-based systems [Dennis 66]. It provided the step from descriptors to more generalized addressing. It is difficult to tell how radical the fundamental concepts were when compared to systems like the Basic Language Machine, which was never completely described in the literature. Is it just a matter of terminology? This issue is discussed in Iliffe's letter to the Surveyors' Forum in the September 1977 issue of *ACM Computing Surveys* (Volume 9, Number 3) and in Dennis' response.

The Chicago and CAL-TSS efforts, while not resulting in finished products, did provide much insight about the design of capability systems. Fabry's paper [Fabry 74], based on his thesis [Fabry 68], is a detailed discussion of the advantages of capability addressing over traditional segmented addressing of primary memory. The paper by Lampson and Sturgis [Lampson 76], in addition to its technical description of CAL-TSS, provides an excellent discussion of the pitfalls of ambitious research projects.

The Plessey 250 computer. (Courtesy Plessey Telecommunications Ltd.)

The Plessey System 250

4.1 Introduction

The second attempt to build a capability-based hardware addressing system was made by the Plessey Corporation in the United Kingdom. Plessey's System 250 [England 72a, England 74], examined in this chapter, was not only the first operational capability hardware system but also the first capability system sold commercially.

Initially the Plessey 250 was not designed as a capability system. Maurice Wilkes of the University of Cambridge had learned about capabilities during several visits to the University of Chicago and had included a capability description in his book on timesharing systems [Wilkes 68]. Wilkes sent a draft of his book to Plessey's Jack Cotton who incorporated capability concepts into the System 250. Because of the strong resemblance between the System 250 and the Chicago effort, Bob Fabry (who had worked on the Chicago Magic Number Machine) later acted as a consultant for Plessey.

Unlike the systems examined thus far, the Plessey 250 was not intended to be a general-purpose timeshared computer. Instead, it was designed as a highly reliable, real-time controller for a new generation of computerized telephone switching systems [Cosserat 72, Halton 72]. The reliability goal was very stringent: mean time between failures of 50 years [Hamer-Hodges 72]. Meeting this goal required that the system be easily configured, tested, and modified while operating in the field. Service improvements or performance upgrades would have to be performed while the system was operational. Such needs led to a multiprocessing design that allowed connection of many processors and memories, as well as traditional and specialized I/O devices.

Although capabilities were used primarily for memory addressing and protection in the Plessey 250, the designers viewed the capability mechanism as a means of restricting the effects of faulty hardware and software components. Fault isolation was a major concern in a multiprocessing environment where several processors had access to a shared memory. One faulty processor could potentially damage another processor's computation. Capability addressing facilitated sharing among processors, while also restricting each processor's domain to the segments for which it possessed capabilities. The Plessey 250's designers also found that capabilities were useful in structuring the operating system [England 72b, Cosserat 74]. Layering and data abstraction were important aspects of the Plessey operating system design.

4.2 System Overview

The multiprocessing architecture of the Plessey 250 allows connection of up to eight processors with up to eight storage modules through separate per-processor data paths. Each storage module consists of up to 64K 24-bit words. Multiprocessing is symmetric, and any processor can perform any function if another processing component fails. Peripherals are connected and controlled through interfaces that allow the addressing of devices as memory. That is, device registers can be read and written by standard LOAD and STORE instructions, and no special I/O instructions are needed.

The Plessey 250's hardware and operating system support a segmented memory space. A segment can contain capabilities or data, but not both. The system has a general register architecture with eight 24-bit data registers (D0-D7) and eight 48-bit capability registers (C0-C7). To access data in a memory segment, a program must load one of the capability registers with a capability for that segment. Programs can freely copy capabilities between capability segments and capability registers using standard hardware instructions.

4.3 Capability Addressing

A Plessey 250 capability permits its possessor to access an object in the system, where an object is a logical or physical resource. The most basic object is a memory segment, and hardware instructions can operate directly on segments through segment capabilities. Capabilities can be stored in capability segments or capability registers, as noted above. For each program, one of its capability registers (C6 by convention) points to a *Central Capability Block* for the program. The Central Capability Block is a capability segment that is the root of a network of program-accessible segments. The closure of this network completely defines the program's execution domain.

A capability in the Plessey 250 has two formats, depending on whether it is stored in a capability segment or a capability register, as shown in Figure 4-1. When stored in a 48-bit capability register, a capability contains three fields:

- A *base address*, which contains the primary memory location of the segment. (The high-order bits specify the storage module or interface, and the low order bits specify the storage element within the module or interface.)
- A *limit*, indicating the size of the segment.
- An *access rights* field, specifying the type of operations permitted on the segment by the owner of the capability. (The six unary-encoded access rights are: execute, write data, read data, enter capability, write capability, read capability.)

This 48-bit capability format, which includes a memory address and limit, is used only when capabilities are loaded into capability registers. When stored in a capability segment, a capability is 24 bits and contains only the access rights field and an index into a central system data structure, the *System Capability Table* (SCT). Each processor has an internal register that contains the address of the SCT. The SCT, which corresponds to the CAL-TSS Master Object Table, holds the base and limit information for all memory segments. In this way,

8	16	
Rights	SCT index	Capability

	Base address	Capability
Rights	Limit	register

Figure 4-1: Plessey System 250 Capability Formats

67

physical addressing information is centralized and relocation of segments is simplified. There is one SCT entry for each object in the system. Because access rights for an object are stored in the capabilities, different processes can possess capabilities permitting different access rights to the same segment.

A program executes a LOAD CAPABILITY instruction to transfer a capability from a capability segment to a capability register. Figure 4-2 shows how the capability register is formed. The hardware first examines the SCT index in the specified capability in memory. This index selects the SCT entry for the segment, which is three words in size and contains a 24-bit checksum and some special flag bits in addition to the base and length fields. The 48-bit capability register is then constructed from the rights field in the capability and the base and limit information found in the selected SCT entry. The capability segment from which the capability is loaded must itself be addressed by a capability register, as shown in the top left portion of Figure 4-2.

When a program loads a capability register, the SCT index from the loaded capability is saved in a process-local data structure called the *Process Dump Stack*. The dump stack is a two-part process data structure containing fixed space for copies of data and capability registers, and a stack used to save information on procedure invocations. When a program executes a STORE CAPABILITY instruction to move a capability from a register to a capability segment, the saved SCT index is used, along with the rights field in the register, to construct the capability

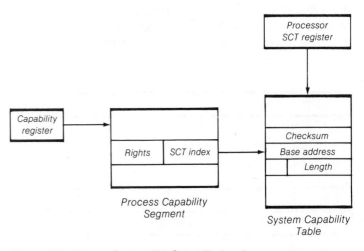

Figure 4-2: Plessey System 250 Capability Loading

in memory. The Process Dump Stack is thus used to hold the SCT index for each capability stored in the eight capability registers.

Because the SCT is shared by all of the processors, the relocation of a segment or the modification of any SCT entry must be synchronized. If several processors try simultaneously to modify a single SCT entry, the entry could be placed in an inconsistent state. In order to prevent this, the Plessey 250 has a facility to trap programs accessing a particular entry. Thus, a processor updating an SCT entry can prohibit other processors from using the entry until the modification is complete.

4.4 Capability Register Usage

Of the eight general-purpose capability registers, several have reserved uses. The first five capability registers, C0-C4, can be freely used by the program to address any memory segments to which the program has access. Register C5 points to a data structure used to store dynamically allocated elements associated with the current process execution. C6, as has been mentioned, contains a pointer to the process's Central Capability Block. This block defines all of the instruction, data, and capability segments associated with the current process. Register C7 contains a capability for the currently executing code segment.

In addition to the eight program-accessible capability registers, each processor has five special-purpose capability registers. These registers hold capabilities that address the following segments:

- The Process Dump Stack that contains backup register values.
- The System Capability Table that contains base/limit values for all storage segments in memory.
- The Start-up Block used for restarting the system after failures.
- The System Interrupt Word that indicates what devices need attention.
- The Normal Interrupt Block that contains device interrupt information.

4.5 Inform and Outform Capabilities

The Plessey 250 operating system provides a virtual segment interface to programs; that is, a program can address its segments independent of whether they are located in primary or secondary memory. Secondary storage is totally transparent to the program. The operating system determines which segments are held in primary memory and which are held on disk storage. When a program attempts to access a segment that is not in primary memory, a trap occurs and the operating system then loads the segment from disk.

Each segment has an associated disk address that is assigned when the segment is created. A segment's disk address is used as its unique identifier, because two segments cannot have the same disk address. When a program creates a new segment, the operating system assigns the secondary storage address for the segment, allocates an SCT entry for the segment, and returns a capability for the segment to the program. The operating system initializes the SCT entry to indicate that no primary memory has been allocated. When the program first attempts to reference the segment, a trap occurs and the operating system allocates primary memory and stores the memory address in the SCT entry.

Because all segments on the Plessey 250 are potentially long-lived, the SCT could grow to enormous size if it had to address every segment in existence. To constrain the size of the SCT and maintain high memory utilization, the Plessey operating system allows SCT entries to be reallocated. At different points in its lifetime, an object may be addressed by different SCT entries. If a segment has not been referenced for a long period of time, the segment can be moved to secondary memory (an operation known as *passivation*), and its SCT entry can be used to address a newly created segment. Later, if the passivated segment is needed, it can be returned to primary memory and an SCT entry (most likely a different one) is allocated.

Reallocation of SCT entries is complicated by the fact that capabilities in memory contain SCT indices. If a segment's SCT entry is reallocated while capabilities for that segment are still in use, those capabilities would erroneously address a different segment. Thus, an object's SCT entry cannot be changed as long as capabilities that address the object are in memory.

To allow SCT entries to be reallocated, the Plessey operating system uses a different format for capabilities that are stored on disk. Capabilities in primary memory are known as *inform* or *active* capabilities; these capabilities contain an SCT index. Capabilities in secondary memory are known as *outform* or *passive* capabilities; each of these capabilities contains a unique identifier, which is the object's disk address. When a capability segment is moved from primary to secondary memory (or the reverse), the operating system changes the form of all the capabilities in that segment.

By changing capabilities from inform to outform, the operating system reduces the number of active references to the SCT. When a segment is passivated, its SCT entry is retained as long as active capabilities exist for that segment. If a segment stays passive for a long time, it is likely that the capabilities for that segment will eventually be passivated also, allowing the SCT entry to be reused. A special operating system process, called the garbage collector, periodically searches the capabilities in primary and secondary memory. The garbage collection process will cause an SCT entry to be deallocated if no active capabilities exist for that entry or will cause an object to be deleted if no capabilities exist at all for that object.

4.6 Instructions and Addressing

A Plessey 250 instruction occupies a 24-bit word and is represented in one of two formats, as shown in Figure 4-3. The first bit of the instruction selects the instruction mode. *Store mode* instructions are used to access storage locations. The instruction specifies a capability register addressing the segment, a 9-bit offset into the segment, and an optional index register

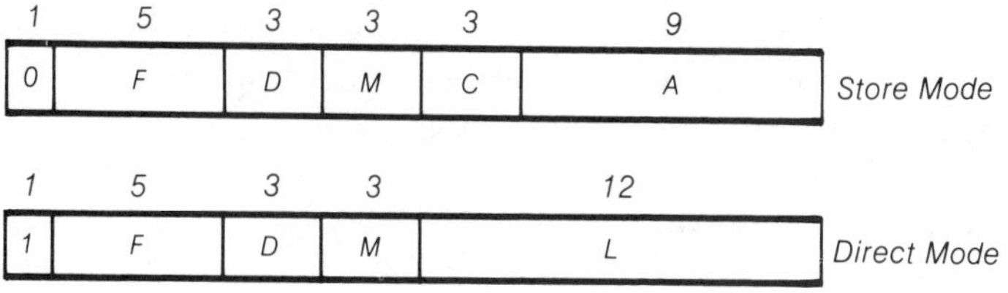

1	5	3	3	3	9	
0	F	D	M	C	A	Store Mode

1	5	3	3	12	
1	F	D	M	L	Direct Mode

F   Function (operation code).

D   Data register.

M   Data register to be used as address modifier (index).

C   Capability register.

A   Address offset.

L   Signed literal (if L = 0 then M defines the second register of a
     two-register instruction).

Figure 4-3: System 250 Instruction Formats

71

modifier. The primary memory address for the operation is calculated by adding the base address contained in the capability register to the sum of the 9-bit literal and the index register contents. This address is validated using the limit field in the capability; the type of access requested is verified against the capability access rights field. *Direct mode* instructions do not require memory access and are used for loading a 12-bit literal or for register-to-register operations.

4.7 Protected Procedure Calls

The Plessey 250 System, unlike most traditional computers, has no privileged mode of operation. The operating system relies only on the protected procedure mechanism for its protection. This mechanism is available to any process and allows a process to add to the facilities supplied by the standard operating system.

A protected subsystem is built by creating a Central Capability Block in which the subsystem will execute. The Central Capability Block serves the same function for the subsystem as for any process: it contains capabilities for code, data, and capability segments available to the executing process. Some of the capabilities in the Central Capability Block are *execute* capabilities for the procedures that implement subsystem services. To make these procedures accessible, the subsystem passes an *enter* capability for its Central Capability Block to appropriate users. The possessors of the enter capability can call any of the procedures defined by execute capabilities in the block, but cannot access capabilities in the block.

To call a protected procedure, a process executes a CALL instruction, specifying an enter capability for a Central Capability Block and an offset in that block. The offset must locate an execute capability for a procedure to be called. The CALL instruction saves the instruction pointer and registers C6 and C7 (defining the Central Capability Block and Current Code Block) on the Process Dump Stack. Register C6 is then loaded with a capability for the Central Capability Block specified in the call; the C6 capability is given *read* access, permitting the called procedure access to *any* of the objects addressed by the central block. Register C7 is loaded with the capability for the instruction segment containing the procedure specified in the call.

Thus, the called procedure executes in its own domain as defined by its Central Capability Block. It is protected from the caller, and the caller is protected from the procedure. A RETURN instruction restores the process to the previous domain by restoring the state of C6, C7, and the program counter from the stack.

4.8 Operating System Resource Management

The Plessey 250 operating system is constructed as a set of protected subsystems that manage various types of *resources*. A segment is one type of resource that users can create and manipulate through capabilities. Other logical resources, such as files and interprocess communication ports, are also accessed by capabilities. Unlike segment capabilities, which are operated on by hardware instructions, logical resource capabilities are enter capabilities that allow the user to request services for the resource.

The resources supported by the Plessey 250 operating system are:

- storage segment
- process
- user
- job
- text file
- symbol directory
- data stream
- synchronizing flag

The last resource type listed, the synchronizing flag, is used both for interprocess communication and for synchronization. Processes that share capabilities for a flag can send messages to the flag or wait for message reception. At any point, a flag can have either a message queue or a queue of processes waiting for new messages. Processes can also wait on multiple flags for one of several events to be posted.

Users gain access to operating system services through a *Central Facilities Block* that contains enter capabilities for system resource allocation routines. Using these routines the caller can create any of the supported system resources. The creation routine returns an entry capability for the resource that can be used to manipulate it.

The actual representation of a resource is defined by the Central Capability Block pointed to by the enter capability returned to the user. The Central Capability Block contains execute capabilities for procedures that manipulate the resource.

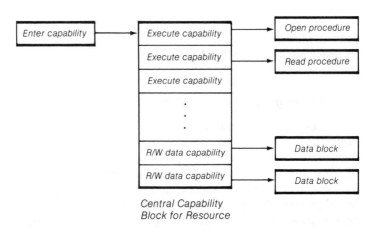

Central Capability
Block for Resource

Figure 4-4: Protected Procedure Resource Subsystem

It also holds capabilities for segments that contain data structures describing the state of the resource. For example, Figure 4-4 shows a Central Capability Block created for a single file object. The Central Capability Block contains capabilities for file procedures and capabilities for file data segments. Note that a separate Central Capability Block will exist for each resource (e.g., file) in the system; however, all resources of the same type will share the same code segments.

4.9 Input and Output

The use of capabilities in the Plessey 250 I/O system is similar to capability usage in storage accesses. Input/output devices are controlled by special device registers that exist in the physical address space. To access device registers, a process must have a capability for that memory space. For each device, one device driver process possesses capabilities for the device registers. This process can execute on any processor and still perform its I/O functions.

Any processor must be able to handle device initiation and completion. Because of this requirement, standard interrupts are abandoned in favor of a polling scheme using shared memory. Approximately every 100 microseconds, each processor examines certain I/O status words that are addressed through two of the five special capability registers (the System Interrupt Word and Normal Interrupt Block). The contents of these locations indicate whether or not any action needs to be taken and on behalf of what device. Other processors must be locked while the examination is made.

Several facts make the Plessey System 250 an important computer system:

1. It is the first functioning computer to use capability addressing.
2. It is the first capability-based computer produced by a commercial manufacturer.
3. It is designed to meet critical real-time performance and reliability needs.
4. It applies capabilities to a multiprocessor environment.

The Plessey 250 is similar to both the Chicago Magic Number Machine and the CAL-TSS system. The use of capability registers as user-loadable segment/base registers is borrowed from the Chicago project, while its addressing resembles the CAL-TSS mechanism. When combined, these features result in a capability design with the following attributes:

1. When stored in user segments, capabilities do not contain physical addresses, but instead contain an index into a central mapping table.
2. Capabilities can be stored on disk and are converted to a different form when copied to disk.
3. A segment is represented by a unique identifier, which allows conversion between inform and outform capabilities.

Because capabilities in primary memory do not contain physical mapping information, they are small and can be compactly stored. Only when a capability is loaded into a register is it expanded to full 48-bit form. The disk address and disk number for a segment provide a unique name for the segment. Capabilities stored on disk contain a unique name, while capabilities stored in primary memory contain a table index. Plessey addressing differs from the CAL-TSS scheme, in which both the capability and the Master Object Table entries contain a segment's unique identifier.

Primary memory addresses are only stored in the SCT and in the capability registers of executing processes. When an executing process is pre-empted, its capability registers are not saved. The Process Dump Stack contains the SCT index and access rights for each capability register, from which the register can be regenerated when the process is activated. Therefore, to relocate a memory segment, the operating system need only search the System Capability Table and the current process capability registers for any active segment addresses.

75

The decision to handle virtual segments and provide a mechanism for storing capabilities on disk greatly simplified the design task and avoided many problems encountered in the CAL-TSS system. The system does not need special naming mechanisms for short-term objects that have second-rate status. All objects are potentially long-lived. Allowing long-lived objects makes garbage collection a necessity, and the Plessey system has a background process responsible for deallocating storage for segments with no remaining capabilities to address them.

The Plessey 250 uses capabilities to simplify multiprocessing. All processors in the system share a single primary memory space. A single table shared by all processors, the System Capability Table, contains primary memory addresses for all segments. Because a process's address space is defined by capabilities that refer indirectly to this table, a process can address its segments from any processor. No special action is required on the part of a processor to initialize a process's memory environment.

Capabilities also aid software error detection. Each process possesses capabilities for only those segments absolutely needed for its function. A process cannot address data outside of its domain; therefore, any errors are limited to that domain. Errors are frequently caught by the addressing mechanism, either as illegal accesses or segment length violations.

A new concern created by capability addressing is the maintenance of capability integrity. On a standard virtual memory system, for example, a 1-bit error in the transmission of a process virtual address is not likely to affect data outside the scope of the process. An error in the transmission of a capability, however, can affect any process in the system. Thus, all hardware involved in holding or transferring capabilities must be error-checked carefully.

The Plessey System 250 combines hardware and software support to provide a uniform view of system resources. All resources are addressed by capabilities; hardware executes operations directly on segment resources while software executes operations on other resources. From a program's point of view, all resources are addressed and manipulated in the same way. In the Plessey resource model, each resource in the system is represented by a Central Capability Block and addressed by an entry capability. The Central Capability Block defines the data segments that contain the state of the resource and the procedures that can manipulate the resource. Procedures are shared among all instances of objects of the same type. The entry

capability to a resource's capability segment permits calling of
the resource manipulation procedures, but prohibits direct
access to the resource data segments.

Because the operating system is implemented as a collection
of resources and protected procedures, it is relatively easy to
extend the operating system in a uniform manner. New protected procedures can be created and addressed through the
System Capability Table. Such procedures can make new types
of resources available to programs.

As implemented, the Plessey 250 protected procedure call
has one weakness. Although a protected procedure call causes
a domain change, the called procedure still has access to any
capabilities left in registers C0 through C4 by the caller. Like-
wise, the capabilities left in these registers by the called procedure when it returns are available to the caller, presenting a
potential security violation. The tradeoff is one of performance, because the registers are an efficient mechanism for passing parameters between a calling and called procedure. Procedures concerned with information leakage can explicitly clear
these registers; however, that is an unusual burden to place on
the caller of a procedure.

Finally, the Plessey 250 system integrates capability usage
into the I/O system in a consistent manner. This is possible
because of the memory-like nature of the I/O interface and
because of the requirement for processor-independent I/O.
However, since I/O devices are forced to be slaves, their power
is limited and additional strain is placed on the processors
using them.

The Plessey System 250 was not meant to be a general-
purpose multi-user computer system but, rather, was intended
for a very specific product area. The targeting of the product to
a limited role probably provided the key to any success the
System 250 has had—its simplicity. The Plessey 250 uses a
small number of simple mechanisms to provide for protection
from and isolation of failure. The Plessey System 250 is still in
use today in military communications systems in the United
Kingdom.

4.11 For Further Reading

The principal descriptions of the Plessey System 250's hardware and software are provided by [England 72b, England 74]
and [Cosserat 74]. Several papers on Plessey 250 can be found
in *The Proceedings of the International Conference on Computer
Communications*, October 1972, and in *The Proceedings of the
International Switching Symposium*, June 1972.

The Cambridge CAP Computer

5.1 Introduction

In 1970, Roger Needham and Maurice Wilkes at Cambridge University began a research project to construct a capability-based machine. In contrast to the Chicago and Plessey designs, which included program-loadable capability registers, Needham and Wilkes' design made registers invisible to the programmer. That is, the machine contained a set of internal registers that the hardware would automatically load when a program specified a capability. Fortunately, the construction of this machine was simplified by several events that had occurred in the years since Wilkes' trip to observe the development of the Chicago Magic Number machine. First, it was possible to build reliable hardware from off-the-shelf TTL components. Second, and more important, it was possible for the computer to contain a reasonably large micro-control storage. The micro-control storage was used to implement the implicit loading of capabilities.

The result of the project, the CAP computer, has been operational at Cambridge since 1976. CAP (not an acronym) is a fully functional computer with an operating system, file system, compilers, and so on. The CAP system is the subject of many papers and a book [Wilkes 79], and the design decisions are the topic of Robin Walker's thesis [Walker 73].

5.2 Hardware Overview

The basic CAP CPU consists of a microprogramming control unit, 4K 16-bit words of micro-control storage, and an arithmetic unit. The CPU contains a 64-entry capability unit that holds *evaluated* capabilities, that is, capabilities and the primary memory locations of the segments they address. These 64 capability unit entries are the registers implicitly loaded by the microprogram. The CAP CPU also contains a 2 x 256-entry cache and a 32-entry write buffer for performance enhancement. All CAP I/O, with the exception of a single control terminal and paper tape, is performed by an associated minicomputer.

CAP's memory is organized into segments up to 64K 32-bit words in size. A segment can contain data or capabilities, but not both. Although a process can address up to 4096 segments, an executing procedure can access a maximum of 16 capability segments at any time. A protected procedure mechanism allows different procedures to access different capability segments. The CAP system provides 16 general-purpose 32-bit registers, B0 through B15, for arithmetic and addressing; these registers cannot be used to hold capabilities. Register B15 contains the current instruction address; B0 is a read-only register that always contains zero. A single accumulator, capable of holding an 8-bit exponent and 64-bit mantissa, is available for floating point computation. In general, arithmetic functions operate on 32-bit integer or floating point values.

CAP's instruction set includes over 200 instructions. Both binary and floating point arithmetic are supported, as well as a variety of logical and control instructions, and a small set of capability manipulation instructions.

5.3 CAP Process Structure

A process is the basic execution and protection entity in the CAP system. A process is defined by a set of data structures that describe a collection of accessible segments and other resources. CAP objects are addressed through capabilities contained within a process's capability segments. Each executing procedure in the CAP system operates within the context of a process.

Like previous capability-based designs, the CAP system provides a process tree structure, as shown in Figure 5-1. The process structure is supported by an instruction that creates subprocesses and an instruction that requests service from a parent process. At the root of the tree is a process called the *Master Coordinator*. The Master Coordinator controls all system hardware resources, which it allocates among level-2 user

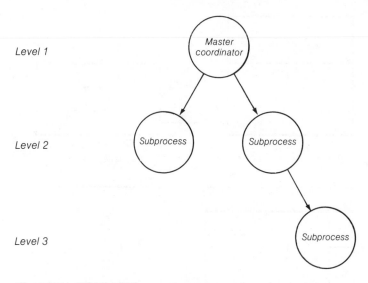

Level 1

Level 2

Level 3

Figure 5-1: CAP Process Hierarchy

processes. Each level-2 user process can, in turn, create further subprocesses, acting as a coordinator for them.

CAP's designers chose to use the process tree mechanism to eliminate the need for a privileged mode of operation. Each CAP process can control the addressing environment and execution of its subprocesses without special privilege or operating system intervention. The desire to provide a very general process tree structure led to a design that closely linked addressing to process structure. This facility was probably overemphasized in the design and only two levels are actually used: the Master Coordinator at level 1 and the user processes at level 2.

5.4 CAP Addressing Overview

A high-level view of CAP addressing is useful before delving into the detailed mechanism. As mentioned, addressing and process structure are intimately related on the CAP system. Figure 5-2 shows the addressing relationship between a process and its subprocess. Two objects of interest are pictured for each process: a capability segment and a data structure called the *Process Resource List* (PRL).

On CAP, a process must possess a capability for any object to be accessed. Capabilities are stored in capability segments. In contrast to the Plessey and CAL-TSS designs, in which capabilities refer to entries in a system-wide table, capabilities

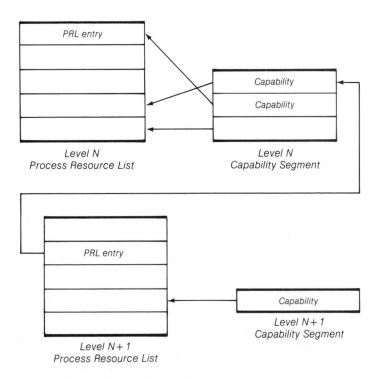

Figure 5-2: CAP Process Addressing

on CAP refer to entries in a process-local table, the Process Resource List. The Process Resource List differs from previous schemes in another important way. PRL entries do not contain primary memory addresses, but instead refer to capabilities *in capability segments of the parent process*. This upward indirection is shown in Figure 5-2 by the arrow leading from the level N+1 PRL entry to the level N capability segment. Indirection continues from there to the level N Process Resource List, and so on, until the Master Coordinator is reached at the top of the tree. The Master Coordinator's Process Resource List contains the primary memory address for each segment.

The following sections describe this addressing structure in more detail, but the reason for the extra indirection is worth noting here: it provides a process with the freedom to control its subprocesses. In the CAP system, a process can directly write the PRL and capability segments of its subprocesses. In this way, a process can dynamically control the addressing environment of its inferiors without operating system intervention. Permitting a process data access to its subprocesses' capability segments does not violate the protection system because of the indirection in addressing. Ultimately, all capabilities and PRL entries in a subprocess must refer to valid capabilities held by its parent process. Therefore, although a parent process can create capabilities for its offspring, these capabilities can only address objects that are accessible to the parent.

5.5 Capabilities and Virtual Addresses

Within a CAP process, an executing procedure addresses segments through capabilities stored in its capability segments. Capabilities can be specified by CAP instructions and manipulated in controlled ways by user programs. Figure 5-3 shows the CAP capability format. As described above, each capability refers to one entry in the Process Resource List. Each capability also contains a type field in the two high-order bits that differentiates segment capabilities, enter capabilities, and so on. The bits marked W and U are set by hardware to indicate that a segment has been written or accessed, respectively.

The encoding of the access field is shown also in Figure 5-3. CAP permits read and/or write access to a capability segment, or read, write, and/or execute access to a data segment. Write capability access permits a process to execute instructions to move capabilities to a segment; it does not allow data operations on the segment. The base, size, and access fields in a capability can be used to *refine* access to a segment defined by a PRL entry. For example, a program can create a new capability with read-only access to a segment for which the PRL permits read/write access. Or, using base and size, a capability can be refined to address only a contiguous subset of a segment. The REFINE instruction performs these operations.

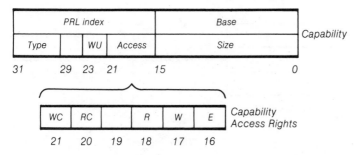

Figure 5-3: CAP Capability and Access Rights Formats

To reference a word in memory, the CAP programmer must specify a capability for a segment and the offset of the word within that segment. The capability is specified by an index in one of the 16 capability segments. A complete CAP virtual address, then, consists of three parts: a capability segment number, a capability index, and an offset into the selected segment.

Figure 5-4 shows the format of a CAP virtual address when stored in memory or a general register. The upper 16 bits of the address are known as the *segment specifier* because they select a capability for the addressed segment. The segment specifier consists of two values: I, the number of one of the 16 capability segments, and F, the index of a capability within that segment. The capability selected in Figure 5-4 contains the index of PRL entry M, which points to a data segment (although the addressing is indirect). The value K in the virtual address is the offset of the target word in this data segment.

Note that each capability segment can hold a maximum of 256 capabilities because the capability index field in Figure 5-4

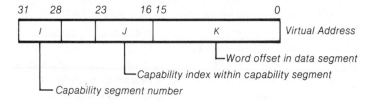

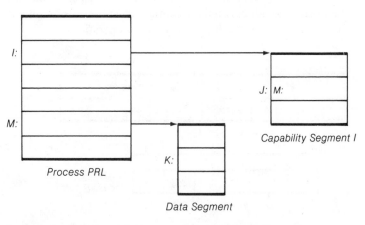

Data Segment

Figure 5-4: CAP Virtual Address

is 8 bits long. There are 16 capability segments, so the process can address a maximum of 4096 capabilities at a given time.

5.6 Process Data Structures

A CAP Process Resource List defines all of the resources available to a CAP process. Figure 5-5 shows the structure of entries in a PRL. A PRL entry is identical in format to a capability, except that the PRL index of the capability is replaced by the segment specifier field. The segment specifier selects a capability in one of the capability segments of the parent process. Just as the base, size, and access fields in a capability can be used to refine the access permitted by a PRL entry, these fields in the PRL entry can be used to refine the access permitted by the parent's capability.

PRL entries resemble capabilities in structure; however, the PRL is not a C-list and differs from a C-list in two important ways. First, PRL entries cannot be manipulated by programs executing within the process. Second, the PRL must contain entries for objects needed by *all* procedures that the process executes. In contrast, most capability systems allow procedures to access private objects not available to the C-list of their caller. Different procedures executing within a CAP process can be restricted to different capability segments and, hence, to different objects; but all of the objects that they collectively address must have entries in the PRL.

In addition to the PRL, each process has a data structure called the *Process Base*, which contains the state of the process. By convention, the first entry in the PRL addresses the Process Base. The first 16 words of the Process Base define the 16 process capability segments by indicating the offset of the PRL entry for each segment, as shown in Figure 5-6. The V bit in each word specifies whether or not that capability segment exists, and the 8-bit offset field indicates which PRL entry

Segment specifier				Base	
Type		WU	Access	Size	
31	29	23	21	15	0

Segment specifier< 31:28> = Parent capability segment
Segment specifier< 23:16> = Index of capability within specified
parent segment

Figure 5-5: CAP PRL Entry

85

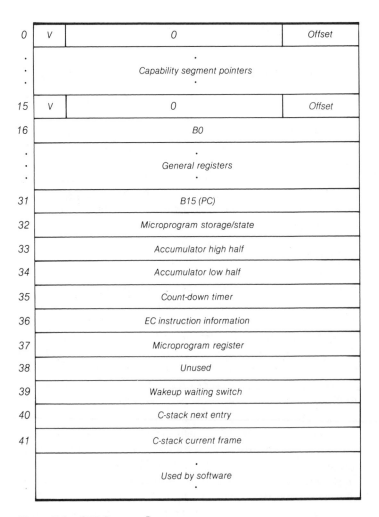

Figure 5-6: CAP Process Base

addresses the corresponding capability segment. All capability segments accessible to a process must, therefore, be addressed through the first 256 PRL entries. The remaining words in the Process Base contain copies of the general registers, a count-down timer, and pointers to the C-stack—a data structure used to save capabilities during procedure invocation.

5.7 Memory Address Evaluation

This section reviews the translation process from virtual address to primary memory location. Because each process owns all segments available to its children, the Master Coordinator at the root of the tree must have capabilities for all segments in the system. In fact, the Master Coordinator is the only process that addresses memory directly. In the PRL of the Master Coordinator, called the *Master Resource List* (MRL), are capabilities similar in format to that shown in Figure 5-5; however, word 0 of these MRL entries contains a memory address in the low-order 20 bits. All capabilities ultimately refer to these MRL entries.

The steps to translating an address are as follows:

1. Locate the specified capability segment in the process, and select the capability in the index contained in the virtual address.
2. Follow the capability link to the entry in the process PRL. Minimize access rights through a logical AND operation, and compute new base and length if required.
3. From the PRL entry, locate a capability in the parent process's capability segment. Once again, apply rights, base, and length minimization.
4. Follow this capability back to the entry in the parent's PRL.
5. Continue this process until the MRL is reached, at which time the physical address can be calculated. Check the offset supplied in the original general address for legality and make the requested reference.

Certain facts are apparent about this mechanism. First, several levels of indirection, and hence, several memory references, are required before an actual operand can be accessed. This problem can be handled with the special hardware that the CAP provides. Second, because capabilities refer to a process-local structure, the PRL, they cannot easily be transferred between processes even at the same level of the hierarchy. Capabilities cannot be copied between processes unless both processes have identical PRLs. Third, capabilities cannot be copied directly from parent to child, but must be passed by constructing PRL entries and corresponding capabilities in the child that refer to the parent capability. Fourth, because of the indirection in both capabilities and PRL entries, a process is totally free to create capability segments and PRL entries for its subprocesses.

5.8 Subprocess Creation

Any CAP process is capable of creating subprocesses to which it can pass access rights to various objects. The creation

87

of a subprocess is accomplished by the ENTER SUBPROCESS (ESP) instruction. One operand of the ESP instruction is a segment that will become the PRL of the new subprocess. Another operand is the index of the PRL entry in that segment for the subprocess's Process Base.

A parent process creates a subprocess PRL by allocating a data segment and constructing PRL entries that refer to the parent's capabilities. Because of the way PRL addressing is implemented, the construction of subprocess PRL entries requires no special privilege. It is impossible for the parent to construct a PRL capability for its offspring that allows it to address an object not addressable by the parent. Since the access rights are minimized at each level during the address evaluation, it is also impossible to increase access rights to an addressable object.

The ESP instruction allows any process to create a subprocess, to define the resources of the subprocess, and to protect itself from the subprocess. Each parent can also service requests from its subprocesses. The subprocess issues an ENTER COORDINATOR (EC) instruction, specifying a code for the operation to be performed. Execution of the EC instruction causes resumption of the parent process at the instruction following the ESP that initiated the subprocess. The code is placed in a general register specified by the original ESP.

Multiprogramming on the CAP system is implemented by using the countdown timer stored in each Process Base. When an ESP instruction is executed, control passes to the subprocess. The subprocess continues execution until either its timer expires or it executes an EC instruction, causing return of control to the parent. The parent process can service the EC or timer expiration, resuming the interrupted process or another subprocess if it likes. The parent might also request service from its own parent via an EC instruction. Before resuming a subprocess by ESP, the parent resets the countdown timer in the process base of the subprocess.

Thus, any process can coordinate the execution of its subprocesses, relinquishing its own allotted processor time for each subprocess to run. In fact, the current process is allowed to run because a set of processes, rooted in the Master Coordinator and terminating with the current process, have each relinquished processor time via ESP. Each process in the list is at a different level of the process tree, and each executes under a time limit specified by its parent. The CAP hardware must, therefore, maintain timers for each level of the process tree because a timer could expire at any level, thereby returning control to the parent of the expiring process.

5.9 The Capability Unit

5.9 The Capability Unit

The CAP capability unit contains storage elements used by the microprogram to enhance system performance. The storage elements include 64 capability registers and 16 tag memory registers, whose use will be described in this section. The principal function of the capability unit is to reduce the effect of CAP's multiple levels of indirection. The capability unit acts as a cache memory (or what is commonly called a translation buffer) for storing recently used segment virtual addresses and their corresponding segment physical addressing information.

Figure 5-7 shows the structure of a capability unit capability register. Each capability register contains information about a segment capability. The base, size, and access fields are used to compute the primary memory address and to validate the attempted memory access. Two tag fields uniquely identify the capability within the capability unit; the segment tag identifies the capability segment that holds the capability, and the capability tag contains the capability's index within that segment. The segment tag is the number of another capability register in the capability unit. Each capability is contained in one of 16 capability segments, and to load a capability into a register, the capability for its capability segment must also be loaded in a register. The number of that register is used as the segment tag field.

8	6	20	16	7	7
Capability tag	Segment tag	Base	Size	Access	Count

Capability tag	Contains the index of this capability within its capability segment.
Segment tag	Identifies the segment containing the capability.
Base	Contains the primary memory address of the segment.
Size	Contains the size of the segment in words.
Access	Indicates the permitted segment access rights.
Count	Contains a count of the number of references to the capability from within the capability unit.

Figure 5-7: Capability Unit Register Format

89

When a program attempts to access a virtual address, the microprogram loads that address into the virtual address register of the capability unit, as shown in Figure 5-8. The capability unit then autonomously attempts to locate the capability register containing the physical attributes of the segment addressed. If the capability is found, the capability unit validates the requested access and performs the primary memory request. If the capability is not found, the capability unit notifies the microprogram, which must then load the needed information into a capability register.

The capability register search uses one of the 16-tag memory registers shown in Figure 5-8. Each of the 16-tag memory registers corresponds to one of the 16-process capability segments. Whenever the microprogram loads a capability for capability segment I into a register, it also loads the number of that register into the corresponding tag memory register. Therefore, tag memory register I specifies the location of the capability for capability segment I in the capability unit. A valid bit in each tag memory register indicates whether or not that register has been loaded.

From the virtual address presented to the capability unit, the unit selects one tag memory register based on the capability segment specifier (the upper 4 bits). The capability unit then uses the tag memory register in an associative search. The capability unit searches for a capability register whose segment tag field matches the contents of the tag memory register. If the tag fields match, then the register contains a capability that is stored in the correct capability segment. The unit must then check the capability index field in the virtual address, shown as J is Figure 5-8, with the capability tag field in the register. If these fields match, the correct segment register has been found. If the J fields do not match, the search continues. The capability unit is able to examine four capability registers at a time during the search.

5.10 Protected Procedures

The protected procedure is the principal CAP protection mechanism. Although other capability systems execute protected procedures in a new process, all procedures called from within a CAP process execute within that same process. However, different procedures may have access to different capability segments and, hence, to different objects. The protected procedure mechanism causes switching of capability segments and, therefore, changes the access domain of a procedure.

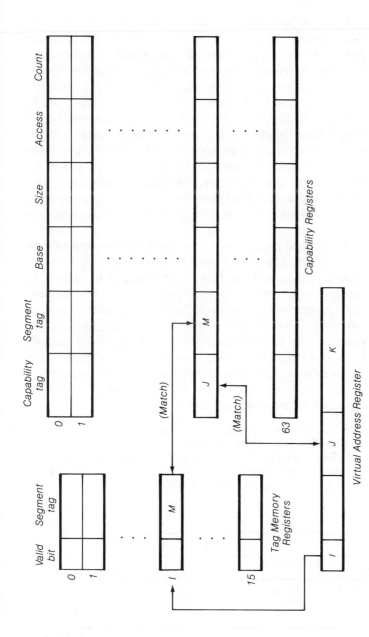

Figure 5-8: CAP Capability Unit

Protected procedures are used extensively both within the CAP operating system and by user programs. All operating system services are programmed as protected procedures, and all compilers output protected procedures. The use of protected procedures to perform system functions is particularly important within the CAP system. Although services could be provided through ENTER COORDINATOR instructions to the Master Coordinator, such instructions would cause a serialization of service. That is, once the Master Coordinator is entered, the service routine would have to complete before another process could execute. By placing operating system services within protected procedures available to every process, several processes can execute service routines simultaneously.

A protected procedure can be called only through an *enter capability* which the caller must possess. Figure 5-9 shows an enter capability and the PRL entry to which it refers. The execution of a protected procedure call causes 5 of the 16 capability segments to be changed. These new capability segments form part of the new domain in which the protected procedure executes. The enter PRL entry shown in Figure 5-9 contains fields that define three of the new capability segments. The creator of a protected procedure is free to use these segments in any way; however, the conventional name and use of the new capability segments are as follows:

A The *argument* capability segment contains capabilities passed as parameters to the currently executing procedure.

N The *new argument* segment is used to construct an argument list for a procedure to be called. This segment becomes the A segment of the called procedure.

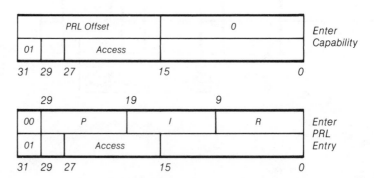

Figure 5-9: CAP Enter Capability and Enter PRL Formats

P The *procedure* segment contains capabilities for code and
   data segments that are shared by all processes executing a
   protected procedure.

I The *interface* segment contains capabilities that are used by
   the procedure but are specific to the executing process, for
   example, a process-local workspace.

R The *resource* segment contains capabilities specific to one
   instance of the protected procedure. For example, the R
   segment might be used to address the representation of an
   object managed by a protected type manager. The representation would be accessible only to the protected procedure.

A program executes an ENTER instruction to call the protected procedure. The single operand to the ENTER instruction
is the location of the enter capability. Parameters are
passed in the N segment. The ENTER instruction then
changes the execution environment, using a data structure
called the *C*-stack to save information about the current procedure. The C-stack is a segment in which the invocation stack
(the procedure-calling record) is maintained. Each procedure
call causes the hardware to place a new invocation frame on the
C-stack by updating the C-stack pointers in the Process Base.
The RETURN instruction restores information placed on the
C-stack, removing the current frame and returning control to
the caller.

In more detail, the ENTER instruction causes the following
events to occur:

- A new C-stack frame is allocated. This 6-word frame is loaded
  with procedure state information, including the PRL indices
  for the current P, I, and R segments.
- The PRL indices for the new P, I, and R segments, stored in
  the enter PRL entry, are used to modify the three words in
  the Process Base that address these three capability segments.
- The PRL index for the current A segment is saved on the
  C-stack. The A segment slot in the Process Base is loaded
  with the PRL index of the current N segment. The Process
  Base slot for the N segment is invalidated.
- The current program counter (B15) is saved on the C-stack.
- The access rights specified by the enter capability and the
  enter PRL entry are ANDed and placed in B14, for examina-
  tion by the procedure.
- The program counter is loaded with the address of the first
  word of the segment addressed by the new P capability.

The protected procedure begins execution at the first word
of the P segment. It executes in the new domain created by the

ENTER instruction and has access to new A, P, I, and R
segments. When the procedure is entered, no N segment
exists. Should the procedure wish to create a new argument
segment for a further procedure call, it executes a MAKEIND
instruction to specify the length of the new N segment. The N
segment is also allocated on the C-stack. Execution of a RE-
TURN instruction destroys the N segment and replaces the previous P, I, R, and A segments.

Each CAP user program is, in fact, a protected procedure,
and is restricted to a subset of the objects addressed by its
process' PRL. This subset is defined by the P, I, and R capability segments made available to the program by its enter capability. Other procedures callable by the program can have
access to different segments. The enter PRL entry for a protected procedure *seals* three capabilities, making them available to the protected procedure when it is called.

The protected procedure mechanism supports the creation
of protected objects and object type managers. For example,
Figure 5-10 shows the implementation of a subsystem supporting protected objects of type *message port*. Each instance of a
port object is represented by a new instance of the port pro-

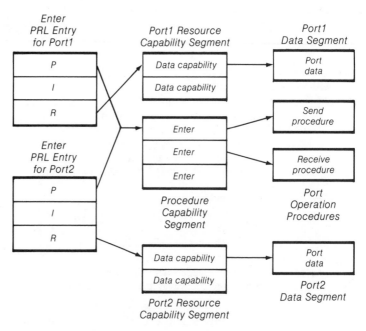

Figure 5-10: CAP Protected Object Implementation

tected procedures. Each instance of the port system contains a pointer to the port protected procedures and a pointer to the segments containing the data structures for one port instance. Figure 5-10 shows enter PRL entries for two ports. Both PRL entries address the same P segment and share the procedures that operate on the ports, but every object has a different R segment that contains the representation of that object instance.

To create a new object, then, the type manager creates an instance of itself with a new R segment. All PRL entries for objects of the same type share a P capability but have different R capabilities for the segments containing the object's representation. Processes are given enter capabilities that address these PRL entries. The type manager defines and interprets the access rights in its enter capabilities. The ENTER instruction makes those access rights easily accessible by placing them in a register.

5.11 Long-Term Storage and Long-Term Names

Like the Plessey 250, the CAP operating system provides for long-term storage of objects. Three types of objects can be preserved on secondary storage: segments, directories, and Procedure Description Blocks. A Procedure Description Block is a segment created by the operating system that defines how a protected procedure should be constructed, including its segments and the capabilities in those segments.

CAP capabilities, like Plessey 250 capabilities, contain the index of a data structure in memory (the PRL). This index is a short-term identifier for an object and is meaningful on the CAP system only during the lifetime of a single process. Therefore, in order to preserve and name objects with a long lifetime, each object must have a unique long-term name. When object names are saved on secondary memory, they must be stored as long-term names.

Each CAP object's long-term name is unique for the life of that object. The long-term name is called the *system internal name* of the object. An object's system internal name is constructed from the disk block address where the object is stored. The CAP operating system maintains a list of all long-term objects that includes the number of references to each object on secondary storage. In addition, the operating system maintains a list for each CAP process that contains the system internal names for all objects addressed by that process's PRL.

Every CAP user has one or more directories in which to store text names of long-term objects and their associated system internal names. Directories are managed by a protected procedure known as the directory manager.

The operating system maintains the storage for an object as long as a reference to that object exists in a directory, in a Procedure Description Block, or in the PRL of an executing process. When a process requests an object from a directory, the system first checks the process-local system internal name list to see if that object is currently in memory. If so, the process will already have a PRL entry addressing the object and a capability can be constructed. Otherwise, the system's long-term system internal name list must be consulted and the object fetched from secondary storage. This operation will cause a PRL entry to be allocated, a capability to be constructed, and a notation to be made in the process-local system internal name list.

Protected procedures are stored on secondary memory as Procedure Description Blocks. A protected procedure, as previously described, consists of three capability segments (procedure, interface, and resource) that are made available as the result of an ENTER instruction. These segments contain capabilities that are used by the protected procedure but may be hidden from other process procedures.

When a protected procedure is created, the operating system constructs a Procedure Description Block containing system internal names of the objects accessible to the protected procedure. The operating system returns an enter capability and places an enter PRL entry in the Process Resource List of the creating process. The PRL entry is constructed so that a trap will occur if an ENTER instruction attempts to use that entry. If a trap occurs, the operating system builds the P, I, and R capability segments from the system internal names in the Procedure Description Block. In this way, such segments do not need to be allocated unless the procedure is actually called.

5.12 Discussion

The Cambridge CAP computer is the first successful university-built hardware and software capability system. Unlike previous university efforts, the CAP implementors completed a system that serves both as a research tool and as a useful service facility. The CAP system is interesting because of several design aspects, including the addressing structure and the use of the microprogram and capability unit for implicit capability loading.

The most influential decision made in CAP's design was the choice of a capability protection system based on a process hierarchy. The goal was to allow any process complete freedom to supervise the activities of its subprocesses. The CAP system permits a process to control the processor scheduling as well as the memory resources of its offspring. The ENTER SUBPROCESS and ENTER COORDINATOR instructions operate at any level of the tree, allowing any process to act as a complete coordinator.

CAP's addressing structure permits direct control of subprocess addressing domains by a parent process. In contrast, a parent process on other capability systems must call a supervisor service to place a capability in a subprocess's C-list. On CAP, however, a process can have data access to its subprocesses' capability segments. No protection violation occurs because of the indirection in subprocess capabilities, although this indirection reduces the efficiency of capability addressing.

An additional problem is caused by the local nature of the Process Resource List. Because all capabilities address the PRL, a process-local structure, they cannot be passed easily between processes. CAP capabilities are different from capabilities on previous systems because they do not contain a *global context-independent* identifier. Although each CAP object has a system-wide unique name, a CAP capability contains a PRL index which is a process-local object name.

Following their initial experience, CAP's designers felt that the process tree had been much overemphasized in the design. The generality of a multi-level process structure, while providing conceptual advantages, led to performance and implementation difficulties. Therefore, only two levels of process structure are actually used in the CAP—the Master Coordinator and the level-2 processes. However, the effect of the process tree design on addressing remains.

A more essential CAP mechanism is the protected procedure. Protected procedures are widely used, both within the operating system and by user programs. Most of CAP's operating system is implemented as protected procedures that execute within the domain of each process; this alleviates the bottleneck that would be caused if all services were performed directly by the Master Coordinator.

Protected procedures are also useful for implementing type managers and protected objects. The procedure (P) segment for the protected procedure specifies the protected object management routines, while the resource (R) segment can be used to specify the representation of a single object instance managed by those routines. When a new object instance is created, the type manager creates a new instance of its protected procedure system. This new instance is represented by a new enter capability and enter PRL entry that have access to a new R segment.

Although the protected procedure mechanism supports the creation of protected objects, it is not extensively used for that purpose within the operating system due to the cost of protected procedures. Using this mechanism for protected objects, a new instance of the type manager (that is, a new protected procedure with its enter PRL entry) must be created for every new object. Creation of a new instance of a protected procedure also causes creation of a new Procedure Description Block, which involves both space and time overhead to the system.

A less expensive mechanism is provided by *software capabilities* (not described in the chapter). The operating system uses software capabilities for addressing operating system objects. Software capabilities can be placed in process capability segments and are protected in the same way that segment capabilities are protected. The type field in the capability indicates whether it is a software capability or another type of capability. A protected procedure can return a software capability to a process as proof of object ownership. The bits in a software capability can be defined by the protected procedure and used in any way. However, software capabilities can only be used by operating system protected procedures because they rely on convention to distinguish the type of object addressed by the software capability.

CAP's capability unit serves to reduce the overhead references required for address translation. A memory reference in a level-2 user process requires four overhead references before the word is accessed, because two capabilities and two PRL entries must be read to compute the primary memory address. The capability unit reduces this overhead by caching frequently used segment capabilities and their segment primary memory addresses.

Additionally, the use of tag memory registers and the structure of the capability register tags permit registers to remain loaded over domain changes. That is, when a context switch or protected procedure call occurs, only the tag memory registers

need to be changed. A call to a short protected procedure will
not cause a turnover of registers in the capability store. However, the capability unit requires that a large number of evaluated capabilities be loaded in registers before it can operate.
For example, for each process capability in the capability unit,
the unit must also hold evaluated capabilities for the segment
containing the capability, for the process PRL and Process
Base of the current process, and for the PRL and Process Base
of the parent process. The overhead is significant, and the 64-
register size of the store would make large process trees im-
practical.

Additional overhead always exists in capability management, and this can be seen in light of the CAP addressing
structure. Because capabilities are defined indirectly, a parent
has the ability to modify or invalidate a capability to which a
junior process refers. Using this mechanism, it is possible to
revoke authority to an object previously allowed a subprocess
(and potentially, its juniors). Since the capability unit maintains translated copies of capabilities, however, it is possible
for a change at a higher level in the process tree to be made
while a lower level capability exists in the capability unit along
with its physical address. Therefore, each time a capability in
memory is modified, the capability unit must ensure that no
junior process capabilities are left in the unit that refer indirectly to the modified capability. Although this is analogous to
the operation required on a virtual memory translation buffer
in any virtual memory system, the operation is more frequent
with capabilities because, while users can modify capabilities,
only the operating system can modify process page registers.

The CAP project has been successful for reasons related
both to the structure of the hardware and the amount of useful
software available to its users. Since it became operational, the
CAP system has continued to be a useful research and computation facility at Cambridge University, and the base hardware
has proven flexible enough to allow further experimentation
with capability architecture [Herbert 78a].

5.13 For Further Reading

Much literature is available on the CAP system and its software. A general discussion of capability addressing and the
CAP approach can be found in [Needham 72 and Needham
74]. The best overview of the CAP system is provided in the
paper by Needham and Walker [Needham 77a], the book by

Wilkes and Needham [Wilkes 79], and the thesis by Walker [Walker 73]. The book describes the operating and filing systems as well as the hardware. The filing system is described also in [Needham 77b, Birrell 78]. Performance evaluations of the CAP system can be found in the papers by Cook [Cook 78, Cook 78b].

Since the original CAP design, Herbert has experimented with a new CAP capability architecture implemented by a microprogrammed kernel running on the CAP hardware [Herbert 78a, Herbert 78b, Herbert 79]. A version of [Herbert 79] is reprinted in [Wilkes 79]. Herbert's kernel corrects some of CAP's problems and supports global naming and a form of sealing as described by Redell [Redell 74a].

The Hydra/C.mmp computer. (Courtesy William Wulf.)

The Hydra System

6.1 Introduction

This chapter marks the transition from capability-based to object-based computer systems. Although somewhat subtle, the distinction is one of philosophy. The systems previously described are primarily concerned with capabilities for memory addressing and protection, although they support abstraction and extension of operating system resources as well. The principal concern of the systems discussed in the remaining chapters is the use of data abstraction in the design and construction of complex systems. In these systems, *abstract objects* are the fundamental units of computing. Each system is viewed as a collection of logical and physical resource objects. Users can uniformly extend the system by adding new types of resources and procedures that manipulate those resources.

The subject of this chapter is Hydra, an object-based operating system built at Carnegie-Mellon University. Hydra runs on C.mmp (Computer.multi-mini-processor), a multiprocessor hardware system developed at Carnegie. Hydra is significant because of its design philosophy and the flexibility it provides for users to extend the base system. This flexibility is supported by capability-based addressing.

6.2 Hydra Overview

In the early 1970s, a project began at Carnegie-Mellon University to investigate computer structures for artificial intelligence applications. These applications required substantial processing power available only on costly high-performance processors. At that time, however, relatively inexpensive mini-computers were becoming available. Therefore, the project sought to demonstrate the cost performance advantages of multiprocessors based on inexpensive minicomputers.

The C.mmp hardware was designed to explore one point in the multiprocessor space [Fuller 78]. Its hardware structure differs from conventional multiprocessing systems in the use of minicomputers, the large number of processors involved, and the use of a crossbar switch for interconnecting processors to main memory. C.mmp consists of up to 16 DEC PDP-11 mini-computers connected to up to 32 megabytes of shared memory. The memory is organized in 16 memory banks connected to the processing units by a 16 x 16 crossbar switch.

Hydra [Wulf 74a, Wulf 81] is the operating system kernel for the C.mmp computer system. Hydra is not a complete operating system in the sense of Multics, Tops-20, or Unix™; rather, it is a base on which different operating system facilities can be implemented. For example, Hydra allows users to build multiple file systems, command languages, and schedulers. Hydra was designed to allow operating system experimentation: flexibility and ease of extension were important goals. Experimentation is often difficult with traditional operating systems because new subsystems require change to a privileged kernel. Any error in privileged code can cause a system failure. To avoid this problem, the designers of Hydra built a kernel on which traditional operating system components could be implemented as user programs. This facility has strong implications for the protection system because user programs must be able to protect their objects from unauthorized access.

Two fundamental design decisions that permit experimentation on the Hydra system are:

- the separation of policy and mechanism in the kernel [Levin 75], and
- the use of an object-based model of computation with capability protection.

The separation of policy and mechanism allows experimentation with policy decisions such as scheduling and memory management. Basic mechanisms, such as low-level dispatching, are implemented in the kernel, while scheduling policy for user processes can be set by (possibly multiple) higher-level procedures. Because this part of the Hydra design is not related to the object system, it will not be described here.

Hydra's object model and its implementation are the subject of the following sections.

6.3 Hydra Objects and Types

The philosophy that "everything is an object" is key to the Hydra design. All physical and logical resources available to Hydra programs are viewed as objects. Examples of objects are procedures, procedure invocations (called local name spaces), processes, disks, files, message ports, and directories. Objects are the basic unit of addressing and protection in Hydra and are addressed through capabilities. The Hydra kernel's main responsibility is to support the creation and manipulation of (1) new object types, (2) instances of those types, and (3) capabilities.

Each Hydra object is described by three components:

- A *name* that uniquely identifies the object from all other objects ever created. The name is a 64-bit number constructed from an ever-increasing system clock value and a 4-bit number identifying the processor on which the object was created.
- A *type* that determines what operations can be performed on the object. The type is actually the 64-bit name of another object in the system that implements these operations.
- A *representation* that contains the information that makes up the current state of the object. The representation consists of two parts: a *data-part* and a *C-list*. The data-part contains memory words that can be read or written; the C-list contains capabilities for other objects and can only be modified through kernel operations.

Figure 6-1 shows an example of a Hydra object. Although shown as strings, the object's name and type are actually 64-bit binary numbers. The object's type is the name of another object in the system—a type object. Hydra objects include capabilities as part of their representation. By storing capabilities for other objects in its C-list, an object can be built as a collection of several Hydra objects.

Each Hydra type represents a kind of resource. A *type object* is the representative for all instances of a given resource. It contains:

- information about the creation of new instances of the type (for example, the initial C-list size and data-part size), and
- capabilities for procedures to operate on instances of the type.

105

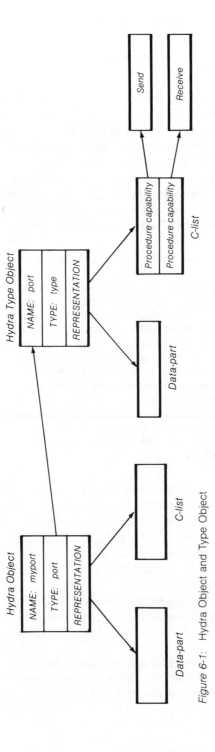

Figure 6-1: Hydra Object and Type Object

PROCESS	The basic unit of scheduling and execution.
PROCEDURE	The static description of an executable procedure.
LOCAL NAME SPACE (LNS)	The dynamic representation of an executing procedure.
PAGE	A virtual page of C.mmp memory that can be directly accessed.
SEMAPHORE	A synchronization primitive.
PORT	A message transmission and reception facility.
DEVICE	A physical I/O device.
POLICY	A module that can make high-level scheduling policy decisions.
DATA	An object with a data-part only.
UNIVERSAL	A basic object with both a C-list and data-part.
TYPE	The representative for all objects of a given type.

Table 6-1: Hydra Kernel-Implemented Types

Thus, the type object is generally responsible for creating new objects of its type and performing all operations on those objects. For example, to create a new message port, the user issues a $CREATE call to the port type object. The port type object creates a new port object, initializes its data-part and C-list appropriately, and returns a capability for the object to the caller. Table 6-1 lists the types directly supported by the Hydra kernel for performance reasons.

To extend the Hydra operating system, users create new type objects that support new kinds of resources. A user creates a new type object by calling the type manager for type objects. Figure 6-2 shows the three-level Hydra type hierarchy. Note that all objects are represented by a type object, including the type objects themselves. The special type object at the root of the hierarchy is called type "type"; that is, both its name and type are "type." This specially designated object is used to create and manipulate type objects.

6.4 Processes, Procedures, and Local Name Spaces

A *process* is the basic unit of scheduling in the Hydra system. There is no explicit process hierarchy; any process can create other processes and pass capabilities for those processes to others. The access rights in a process capability determine what operations can be performed on that process—for exam-

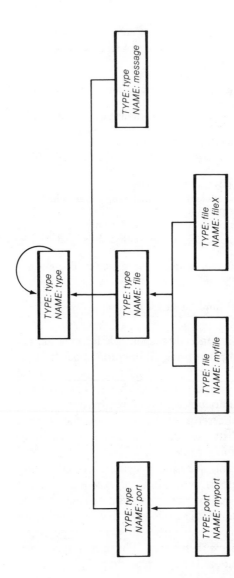

Figure 6-2: Hydra Type Hierarchy

ple, whether it can be stopped and started. A process with suitably privileged capabilities can, therefore, schedule the execution of other processes.

The Hydra protection system is procedure-based rather than process-based. All Hydra procedures are protected procedures that carry their own execution domains. The current domain of a process depends on the procedure that it is executing. The process is the entity in which the procedure is scheduled, and it maintains the chain of procedure calls that have occurred within the process.

To differentiate a procedure from its executing invocations, Hydra supports two object types: the procedure object and the *local name space* object. A Hydra *procedure object* is the *static* representation of a procedure. The procedure object contains instructions, constant values, and capabilities that are needed by the procedure for its execution. The capabilities are maintained in the C-list of the procedure object.

The procedure object is actually a template from which an activation is built when the procedure is called. A procedure is called through a procedure capability. When a procedure call occurs, the Hydra kernel creates a local name space object and initializes it from information contained in the associated procedure object. The LNS is the activation record for the executing procedure; it represents the *dynamic* state of the procedure's execution. Since procedures can be shared, several LNS objects can exist to represent different activations of a single procedure. Hydra allows both recursive and re-entrant procedures.

The LNS defines the dynamic addressing environment for a procedure. All of the objects that can be directly addressed by the procedure must be reachable through capabilities in the C-list of the LNS. The capabilities are initially obtained from two places:

- the called procedure object (these are known as inherited capabilities), and
- capability actual parameters passed by the caller.

Within the executing procedure, capabilities are addressed by their index in the LNS C-list. As the procedure executes, the LNS changes as capabilities are acquired, copied, and deleted.

6.5 Hydra Operations

C.mmp is constructed from PDP-11 minicomputers, which do not support capabilities or virtual memory addressing.

Therefore, all Hydra object operations are performed through calls to the Hydra kernel. A procedure cannot manipulate the data-part of an object with processor instructions. Instead, the procedure performs a kernel operation to copy data from the data-part into its local memory for examination or modification. Another call to the kernel moves data from local memory to the object's data-part. No direct copying is allowed to the C-list.

Since a number of operations are common to objects of all types, the kernel provides a set of *generic operations* that can be applied to any object, assuming the caller has a sufficiently privileged capability. Table 6-2 lists some of these object operations, as well as some of the standard capability operations.

A typical kernel call might specify several parameters that are capabilities. In general, any parameter requiring a capability will also allow a *path* to a capability. The path allows a user to specify several levels of indirection to the target object. The path is specified as a list of C-list indices, leading from a capa-

$GETDATA	Copy data from the data-part of a specified object to local memory.
$PUTDATA	Copy data from local memory to the data-part of a specified object.
$APPENDDATA	Append data from local memory to the data-part of a specified object, extending the size of the data-part.
$MAKEDATA	Create a new data object (data-part only) initialized with N words from a local segment, and return a capability for the new object.
$MAKEUNIVERSAL	Create a new universal object (data-part and C-list) and return a capability for the new object.
$GETCAPA	Copy a specified target capability (e.g., in a specified object's C-list) to the current LNS (local addressing environment).
$PUTCAPA	Copy a capability from the current LNS to a specified object C-list slot.
$APPENDCAPA	Append a capability from the current LNS to a specified object's C-list, extending the C-list size.
$COMPARE	Compare two capabilities.
$RESTRICT	Reduce the rights in a specified capability.
$DELETE	Delete a specified capability.
$CREATE	Create a new object with the same type and representation as another object.

Table 6-2: Generic Object and Capability Operations

64-bit object name	Generic rights	Auxiliary rights

Figure 6-3: Hydra Capability

bility in the current LNS C-list, through a capability in the C-list of the object selected, and so on.

6.6 Capabilities and Rights

Hydra capabilities contain an object's name and access rights. The access rights are divided into two fields: a 16-bit *generic rights* field and an 8-bit *auxiliary rights* field, as illustrated in Figure 6-3. (This figure is somewhat simplified; capabilities have different formats which are shown in detail in Section 6.9.) The generic rights, listed in Table 6-3, can be applied to any Hydra object. In general, they control permission to execute the generic operations listed in Table 6-2. The auxiliary rights field is type specific; its interpretation is made by the procedures that operate on the specific object type.

The rights are single-bit encoded, and the presence of a bit always indicates the granting of a privilege. This convention simplifies rights restriction and rights checking and allows the

GetDataRts, PutDataRts, AppendDataRts	
	Required to get, put, or append data to an object's data-part.
GetCapaRts, PutCapaRts, AppendCapaRts	
	Required to get, put, or append to an object's data-part.
DeleteRts	Allows this capability to be deleted from a C-list.
KillRts	Allows deletion of capabilities from the C-list of the named object. The capability to be deleted in that C-list must have DeleteRts.
ModifyRts	Required for any modification to an object's representation.
EnvRts	Environment rights allows a capability to be stored outside of the current LNS.
UncfRts	Unconfined rights allows an object addressed through a specified object to be modified.
CopyRts	Required to execute the $COPY operation.

Table 6-3: Capability and Generic Object Access Rights

111

kernel to verify that a capability has sufficient generic and auxiliary rights for a specific operation.

A type manager typically has the power, through possession of a special capability, to gain additional privileges to an object of its type passed by a caller. This facility, known as rights amplification, will be described in Section 6.7. In some cases a caller may wish to restrict a subsystem's use of capability parameters and the objects they address. In particular, the user may wish to ensure that a called procedure *does not*:

- modify the representation of an object,
- retain the capability for an object following return of the call, or
- copy information from an object into any memory that could be shared with other programs.

These restrictions can be guaranteed through the use of three special rights listed in Table 6-3: modify rights (ModifyRts), environment rights (EnvRts), and unconfined rights (UncfRts) [Cohen 75, Almes 80].

ModifyRts is required in any capability that is used to modify the representation of an object. For example, in order to write to an object's data-part, the executing procedure must have a capability containing both PutDataRts and ModifyRts. By removing ModifyRts from a capability parameter, a program can guarantee that a called procedure will not modify that object because, unlike the other generic rights, ModifyRts *cannot* be gained through amplification.

EnvRts is required for a procedure to remove a capability from its local name space. When a program removes EnvRts from a capability that is passed as a parameter, it guarantees that no copies of the capability can be retained by the called domain following its return. Without EnvRts, it is impossible for a called procedure to save a capability in a local object's C-list to be used later. Although a capability without EnvRts can be passed to another procedure as a parameter, that procedure will once again find a capability in its LNS without EnvRts and will not be able to save it. EnvRts also cannot be gained through amplification.

Although EnvRts prohibits a procedure from saving a capability, it does not prohibit the procedure from copying all of the possibly confidential information from that object into a new object. UncfRts, when removed from a procedure capability, restricts the storage of information by the called procedure. If a procedure is called using a capability lacking UncfRts, all capabilities copied from the procedure object into the LNS will have UncfRts and ModifyRts removed. That is, the procedure will be forced to execute in an environment in which it cannot modify any of its own objects or any objects reachable through its own capabilities. Therefore, it will not be able to maintain any permanent state following its return. The only objects that can be modified by the call are those passed by capability parameters that contain ModifyRts.

6.7 Supporting Protected Subsystems

A major goal of the Hydra system is the support of the object-based programming methodology. That is, facilities are added to the operating system by creating new object types. A *type manager*, represented by a Hydra type object, is a module that creates new instances of its type and performs operations on those instances. The objective of this methodology is to localize knowledge of the representation and implementation of each type to its type manager. Users can call type manager procedures to create and manipulate objects, but cannot directly access an object's representation.

To support this programming style, a type manager must be able to:

- create new object instances of its type,
- return a capability for a new instance to the caller requesting its creation (this capability identifies the object but must not allow its owner to access the object's representation directly), and
- retain the ability to access the object's representation when passed a capability for an object it created.

The type manager must, therefore, be able to *restrict* the rights in a capability that it returns to a caller and later *amplify* those rights when the capability is returned. The amplified rights permit the type manager to examine and modify the object's representation. Amplification occurs during procedure calls through a special type of capability owned by the type manager called a template.

6.7.1 Templates

There are two common operations that the kernel performs during Hydra procedure calls. First, the kernel verifies that parameter capabilities have the expected type and required

113

rights for the operation implemented by the procedure. Second, the kernel can, under controlled circumstances, amplify the rights passed in a capability parameter. This facility is required to allow subsystems to perform operations on an object that are not permitted to the user of the object.

Both the type checking and amplification facilities are provided through a mechanism called capability *templates*. A template is a kind of capability used by type managers to implement type systems. Templates do not address objects, but give the possessor special privileges over objects or capabilities of a specified type. As the name implies, the template capability is a form used to verify the structure of a capability or to construct a capability. Templates are stored in procedure C-lists and can be manipulated with capability operations. There are three types of templates: parameter templates, amplification templates, and creation templates.

Parameter templates are used to verify the capability parameters passed to a procedure. The procedure object's C-list contains parameter templates as well as capabilities for procedure-local objects. When a procedure call occurs, the kernel builds the LNS C-list from the procedure object's C-list. The procedure's C-list contains its own capabilities that are copied directly to the LNS C-list and parameter templates that represent slots to be filled in with capabilities passed as parameters. The parameter template contains a type field and a required rights field. When copying a capability parameter to the LNS, the kernel verifies that the type matches the template's type field and that the rights in the capability are *at least as privileged* as those required by the template. Special templates can also be provided that will match any type or rights.

The procedure C-list can also contain *amplification templates*. An amplification template contains a type field and two rights fields: required rights and new rights. The type and required rights fields of the amplification template are used to validate the capability parameter in the same way that a parameter template is used. However, once validated, the kernel stores the capability in the LNS with the *new rights* field specified in the amplification template. These rights can either amplify or restrict rights, as specified by the template.

Amplification templates can only be created by the owner of a capability for a type object. In general, only a type object will own the amplification templates for its own type. However, it is possible for a subsystem to own amplification templates for objects of several types. Figure 6-4 illustrates a Hydra proce-

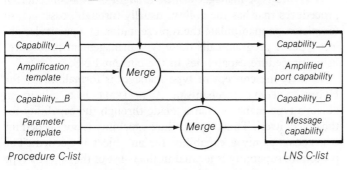

Figure 6-4: Hydra Procedure Call

dure call that uses both parameter and amplification templates. The call sends a message, identified by a message object capability, to a port identified by a port object capability. The call is made to the port type manager that must manipulate the representation of the port object to indicate that a message has arrived. In this example, the C-list of the procedure object contains two inherited capabilities that are copied directly to the new LNS. The procedure C-list has an amplification template that is merged with the port capability actual parameter. The merge operation verifies the type and rights of the capability and stores a capability in the LNS with *amplified* rights. The procedure C-list also has a parameter template that is merged with the message capability parameter. In this case, the merge operation simply verifies the type and access rights of that capability and then copies the capability actual parameter into the LNS.

The third template type, the *creation template*, is not used in the procedure call mechanism, but can be used to create a new instance of a specific type. A creation template contains an object type and rights. Using the $CREATE kernel operation, an object with the specified type and rights can be created. In general, subsystems do not provide creation templates; they require that a user call the subsystem in order to create a new instance. The subsystem then uses its private creation template to create the new instance, which the subsystem initializes appropriately. The subsystem might then restrict some of the rights in the capability returned for the new object and pass that restricted capability to the user.

115

6.7.2 Typecalls

A Hydra type manager can be thought of as a collection of procedures that has the ability, usually through possession of templates, to manipulate the representation of a particular object type. A program calls these type management procedures using procedure capabilities in the current LNS.

In fact, the concept of type manager is formalized by the Hydra TYPECALL mechanism. A TYPECALL is a call to an object's type manager that is made through the capability for the object itself. Thus, a procedure capability is not needed for a TYPECALL; only a capability for an object is needed. The procedure capability is located in the C-list of the object's type manager, which can be found indirectly through the object.

Figure 6-5 shows an example of the TYPECALL mechanism. The TYPECALL invokes the second procedure in the type object for the specified port object. Two parameters are passed to the TYPECALL, the capability for the port object and the capability for a message object. The capability for the port object is listed twice: once as the object through which the TYPECALL is made and once as a parameter to the TYPECALL.

The TYPECALL mechanism supports abstraction in several ways. First, the owner of an object does not need to possess capabilities for its type object or for procedure objects to manipulate that object. In effect, a TYPECALL requests that the object perform an operation on itself. Second, if all objects support a common set of generic operations at identical type indices, a user can find information without knowing an object's type. For example, if all type objects implement a "tell me your type name" operation as the first procedure and "display yourself" as the second, then a user can apply those operations equally on all objects.

6.8 Hydra Object Storage System

A Hydra object, once created, has a lifetime independent of the process that created it. As long as a capability exists for an object, that object will be retained by Hydra and made available when referenced. Hydra stores most long-lived objects on disk when they are not in use and brings them into primary memory when a reference is made. Given a capability for an object, a user can perform any legitimate operation without concern for whether or not the object is currently in primary memory.

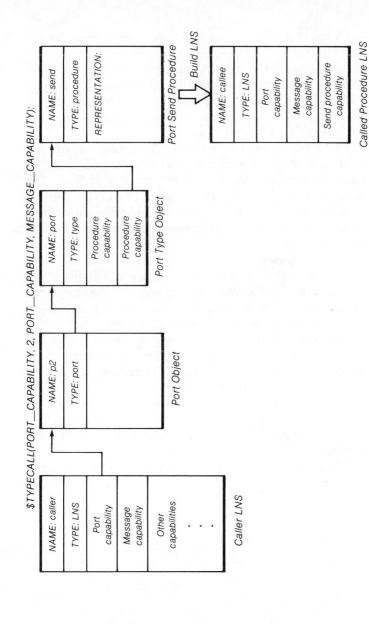

Figure 6-5: Hydra TypeCall

Hydra, thus, provides a uniform single-level object addressing environment to its users. Although objects can be stored in primary or secondary memory, the location of an object is invisible to the Hydra user. The Hydra kernel must, therefore, manage the movement of objects between primary and secondary storage. The mechanism for storing and locating objects is the Hydra *Global Symbol Table*.

The Global Symbol Table (GST) contains information about every object reachable by the kernel. The GST is divided into two parts: the Active GST and the Passive GST. The *Active GST* maintains information about objects stored in primary memory, while the *Passive GST* maintains information about objects stored in secondary memory. An object is said to be active or passive depending on whether it is in primary or secondary memory.

As previously stated, the representation of a Hydra object consists of its C-list and data-part. In addition, the kernel constructs data structures called the *active fixed part* and *passive fixed part* that contain state information for active and passive objects, respectively. Table 6-4 shows the formats of the two fixed parts. As their names imply, the fixed parts have a fixed size for easy storage and access. Many object operations can be satisfied by reference to the fixed part alone, and it is possible for the active fixed part to be in primary memory while the representation is still in secondary memory. In this case, the object's fixed part is said to be active while the representation is passive.

When a new object is created, Hydra stores its representa-

Passive Fixed Part	*Active Fixed Part*
Global Object Name	Global Object Name
Object Flags	Object Flags
Current Version Disk Address	Current Version Disk Address
Previous Version Disk Address	Previous Version Disk Address
Type Name	Total Reference Count
Color (for garbage collection)	Active Reference Count
	Type Object Index
	Checksum of Fixed Part
	State
	C-List Primary Memory Address
	Data-Part Primary Memory Address
	Mutex Semaphore (object lock)
	Time Stamp (of last access)
	Color (for garbage collection)

Table 6-4: Hydra Active and Passive Fixed Parts

tion in primary memory and allocates and initializes an active fixed part. The kernel stores the object's active fixed part in a data structure called the Active GST directory. The Active GST directory is organized as an array of 128 headers of linked lists, as shown in Figure 6-6. Each linked list contains active fixed parts, and the appropriate list for an object's fixed part is determined by a hashing function on the object's 64-bit name.

The division of the Active GST directory into 128 lists serves two purposes. First, it speeds up the GST search, since the linked lists can be kept relatively short. Second, it allows parallelism in the access of the active fixed parts. Only one processor can search a linked list and access a specific active fixed part at a time. By dividing the Active GST into 128 lists, a lock can be maintained separately for each list, allowing simultaneous searches of different lists.

There are two events that cause a Hydra object to be copied to secondary memory. First, *passivation* can be triggered by a kernel process that removes objects from primary memory according to their last reference times. This is analogous to swapping in traditional systems. Second, a program can perform an explicit UPDATE function, requesting that an object's representation be written to disk. In this case, the object remains active with the guarantee that the active and passive copies are identical. The UPDATE operation is used to ensure consistency over system crashes, because any active representation will be lost following a crash. UPDATE is used primarily by type managers.

Two versions of each object are kept on secondary stor-

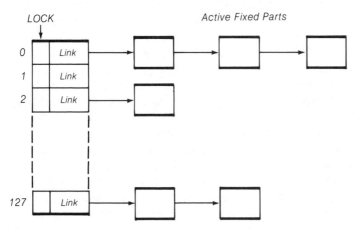

Figure 6-6: Active Fixed Part Directory

119

age—a current version and a previous version. When an object is passivated, its representation is written to secondary storage, destroying the older of the two versions. If any failure occurs during the write operation, the newer version on disk is left intact. Following successful completion of the UPDATE, the newly passivated image becomes the current version, with the former current version becoming the previous version.

Passive objects are stored in the Passive GST. A passive object is stored as a contiguous array of disk blocks containing the passive fixed part, data-part, and C-list. To locate a passive object, a search of the Passive GST directory is made. The Passive GST directory is stored on a high-speed, fixed-head disk and consists of copies of all of the passive fixed parts. The passive fixed parts are organized in 256 blocks for the purpose of synchronization and parallel search. The global object name is used as a key in the search for the correct block.

Object *activation* occurs when the kernel fails to locate a referenced object in the Active GST. The kernel must then search the Passive GST directory. Activation can occur in two phases. First, the object's fixed part is activated. The active fixed part is constructed from information in the passive fixed part. Many operations can be completed with activation of the fixed part alone. Then, if the object's representation must be activated, the C-list and data-part are read into memory.

6.9 Capability Representation

Just as Hydra objects can be active or passive, so Hydra capabilities have both active and passive forms. These forms are shown in Figure 6-7. Active and passive capabilities differ in the format of the object address. An active capability contains the primary memory address of the object's active fixed part, while a passive capability contains the object's 64-bit name. An object reference using an active capability is obviously more efficient, as it does not require a GST search.

An active capability cannot be stored on secondary memory because it contains the primary memory address of the active fixed part, which can be swapped out. When Hydra writes an object to secondary storage, it converts all the capabilities in its C-list to passive form. When Hydra activates an object, it leaves capabilities in passive form until they are used. When a program addresses an object through a passive capability, the kernel searches the GST and converts that capability to active form.

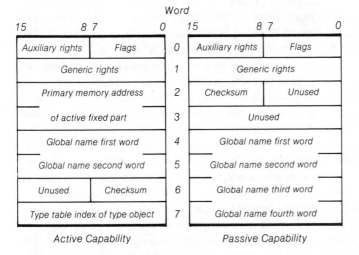

Figure 6-7: Hydra Capability Formats

Because an active capability contains the primary memory address of the active fixed part, an active fixed part cannot be removed from memory as long as active capabilities exist for the object. For this reason, an *active reference count* is maintained in the active fixed part. The active reference count indicates the number of physical addresses that exist for the fixed part. When this count is decremented to zero, the active fixed part (and the object's representation) can be passivated.

6.10 Reference Counts and Garbage Collection

On systems such as Hydra, with long-term object storage, it is difficult to know when an object can be deleted. An object can have many users since capabilities can be freely passed between processes. Users can also delete capabilities, and when no capabilities exist for an object, the object should be deleted. Objects that are no longer reachable are known as *garbage objects* and the general problem of finding them is known as *garbage collection.*

Reference counts can help in the garbage collection problem, and Hydra maintains both an active reference count and a total reference count in an object's active fixed part. The total reference count indicates the total number of capabilities for an object, including passive capabilities in the Passive GST. If the total and active reference counts in an active fixed part become zero, the kernel deletes the object because it can no longer be referenced.

121

Reference counts in themselves are insufficient to stop the accumulation of garbage objects for several reasons. First, reference counts cannot catch object reference cycles. For example, if objects X and Y have capabilities for each other in their C-lists but no other capabilities for X and Y exist, then both objects are garbage and should be deleted. However, both objects will have reference counts of one. Second, because the active and passive fixed parts for Hydra objects are not always consistent, any total reference count maintained in the passive fixed part can be in error following a crash. This inconsistency occurs because it is not feasible to modify the passive fixed part reference count on every capability copy operation.

Because of the insufficiency of reference counts, Hydra includes a parallel garbage collector [Almes 80]. The parallel garbage collector consists of a collection of processes that execute concurrently with normal system operation. The garbage collector scans all objects, marking those that are reachable. The *color* field in the active and passive fixed part is provided for this purpose. Following the marking of objects, another scan is made to locate objects that were not marked—those that are unreachable and therefore are garbage. These objects are deleted.

It is important to note that while the garbage collector is running, capabilities can be freely copied and deleted. The Hydra garbage collector must also cope with the dual residency of objects in the Passive and Active GSTs.

6.11 Discussion

Perhaps the best indication of Hydra's success is that much of its philosophy now seems obvious. The object model and the large single-level object address space have found their way into contemporary products. These ideas did not completely originate with Hydra, nor was their implementation on Hydra totally successful (reflections on the Hydra/C.mmp system by its designers can be found in [Wulf 78 and Wulf 81]). However, the basic philosophy has proven to be a valuable model for system design.

Although previous capability systems provided primitive objects, user-defined objects, and capability addressing, Hydra is the first to present its users with a uniform model of the abstract object as the fundamental system resource. All resources are represented as objects, and objects can be protected and passed from domain to domain. Users can create new resources, represented by type objects, and can control instances of these resources through type-specific procedures.

As the designers point out, the system probably went too far with the flexibility allowed for object protection [Wulf 81]. For example, although direct operations on an object's representation can be restricted to the object's type manager, the protection system allows any user with a sufficiently privileged capability to access the object. To support this generality in a controlled fashion, Hydra defines a large set of generic object rights. In the usual case, however, only the type manager is allowed to access the object, and it must amplify the needed rights through an amplification template. In general, it would be simpler to restrict representation access to type managers who are implicitly given all rights to their objects' representations.

Hydra also attempts to solve some complex protection problems with special rights bits. A caller can prevent a called procedure from modifying an object or "leaking" information from the object. However, it is not always possible for a procedure to operate correctly without some of the special rights (for example, modify rights). Some subsystems may not be able to operate in a confined environment. In addition, it is often difficult for the caller to know what effect the removal of special rights will have on a called subroutine, although good documentation practices can help alleviate this problem.

Many of Hydra's shortcomings are a result of the hardware base, including the small address space and lack of hardware capability support in the PDP-11s. All capability and object operations are executed by operating system software, and even a type manager must copy data from the representation of its objects to local memory for modification. A domain change on Hydra, which requires creation of a new local name space object, type and rights checking of capabilities, and so forth, takes over 35 milliseconds. This severe penalty for a domain change forces a programming style that is contrary to that which is intended. That is, if domain changes are expensive, programmers will tend to use them infrequently and programs will not be written to execute in the small constrained protection domains originally envisioned.

In general, Hydra's objects are too expensive (in terms of space overhead, time for creation, etc.) for their actual usage. Measurements of Hydra show that over 98 percent of all objects are created and destroyed without ever being passivated [Almes 80]. Hydra objects are, therefore, relatively short-lived. The same measurements show that the median object size is 46 bytes for the data-part and 6 capabilities for the C-list. The GST active fixed part overhead for such an object is rather large, as is the cost of each capability.

An important feature of Hydra is the use of large object names—its unique-for-all-time object identifiers. By using a 64-bit value for an object's name, the kernel avoids searching for dangling references when an object is deleted. Although an object's name never changes, capabilities are modified when moved between primary and secondary storage. The change of capability format is simply a performance optimization used to reduce the overhead of Hydra's software-implemented capability support. An operation on an object's capabilities, such as the change from active to passive format, is simplified by the fact that all capabilities are stored in a single C-list.

The Hydra GST is the mechanism for implementing a single-level uniform address space. The single-level address space greatly simplifies a number of problems for both users and the operating system. Most programs do not need to know about the existence of secondary storage. For type managers that must ensure that an object's representation is preserved on secondary memory, Hydra provides the UPDATE operation.

The Hydra developers succeeded in constructing a large, functioning operating system (details of the development can be found in [Wulf 75]). In addition, they were able to implement several useful subsystems outside of the kernel, as intended. These included directory systems, file systems, text editors, and command languages. Perhaps the greatest shortcoming of Hydra, however, was that it did not become a system of choice among programmers at Carnegie-Mellon. Lampson and Sturgis, in their retrospective on CAL-TSS, state the common problem of many operating system research projects:

> ...we failed to realize that a kernel is not the same thing as an operating system, and hence drastically underestimated the work required to make the system usable by ordinary programmers. The developers of Hydra appear to have followed us down this garden path [Lampson 76].

Even so, a tremendous experience was gained from Hydra that has passed to many follow-on systems. The C.mmp hardware was finally dismantled in March 1980; however, still operating at Carnegie-Mellon was a direct descendant of Hydra/C.mmp, which is discussed in the next chapter.

6.12 For Further Reading

The Hydra philosophy was first presented in the original *CACM* paper on Hydra [Wulf 74a]. More recently, Wulf, Levin, and Harbison have written an excellent book on the Hydra system that describes both the kernel and some of its subsystems [Wulf 81]. The book also includes performance measurements of Hydra and the C.mmp hardware. The paper by Wulf and Harbison is a retrospective on the Hydra/C.mmp experience [Wulf 78].

Three papers on Hydra appeared in the *Proceedings of the 5th ACM Symposium on Operating Systems Principles* in 1975. These well-known papers describe the separation of policy and mechanism in Hydra [Levin 75], the Hydra protection system [Cohen 75], and the Hydra software development effort [Wulf 75].

Almes' thesis describes the Hydra garbage collector and also presents measurements of the GST mechanism showing object size and lifetime distributions [Almes 80]. The paper by Almes and Robertson describes the construction of one of several Hydra file systems [Almes 78]. Low-level details of the Hydra kernel and its operations are documented in the *Hydra Kernel Reference Manual* [Cohen 76].

The Cm* computer. (Courtesy Dr. Zary Segall.)

The StarOS System

7.1 Overview of StarOS

Carnegie-Mellon's Hydra/C.mmp project examined the use of multiprocessors in the solution of artificial intelligence problems. C.mmp supported up to 16 processors and memories connected through a crossbar switch. By 1975, however, it was clear that multiprocessors involving hundreds of microprocessors would be possible. The C.mmp crossbar scheme, which increases geometrically in complexity with the number of processing elements, was infeasible for such systems. Therefore, the CM★ project [Jones 80a], started in 1975 at Carnegie-Mellon, took a different approach to interconnection—one that grows linearly in complexity with the number of processing elements. By 1979, the CM★ configuration contained 50 operational processors.

CM★ consists of a large collection of *computer modules*, in which each computer module is a DEC LSI-11 processor with its bus, local memory, and peripherals. A computer module *cluster*, shown in Figure 7-1, is formed by a set of computer modules communicating through a *map bus*. Memory requests generated in each computer module are routed by a switch, either to local memory or to the map bus. The CM★ system consists of a set of clusters connected by an *intercluster bus*. A computer module can issue addresses for local, intracluster, or intercluster memories.

The connection between clusters is managed by a unit called the *Kmap*. The Kmap is a horizontally microprogrammed processor that, in addition to supporting intercluster refer-

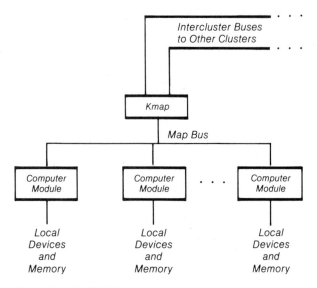

Figure 7-1: A CM* Cluster

ences, is used to execute operating system functions. Performance-critical parts of the operating system, such as capability operations, are therefore implemented in Kmap microcode.

Two operating systems were constructed to support distributed software for CM*: STAROS and Medusa [Ousterhout 80a, Ousterhout 80b]. STAROS, the subject of this chapter, is an object-based operating system that supports the execution of task forces [Jones 78b]. A *task force* is a collection of cooperating processes executing concurrently to perform a single job. Task forces are distinguished from most cooperating process schemes by their dynamic nature. The structure of a task force corresponds to the available resources rather than to the functional requirements and can change with dynamic resource changes.

In general, each of the processes within a task force is small if measured by its resource requirements. A task force process executes within a small domain and interacts with other task force processes for many of its needs. STAROS objects reflect the constrained needs of this environment, and the structure is much simpler than that of Hydra. The following sections take a brief look at object structure and addressing in the STAROS operating system.

7.2 STAROS Object Support

All information in the STAROS system is contained within objects. Each object has a type, and the type defines the operations that can be performed on the object. As with Hydra, objects are addressed by capabilities that name the object and specify the permitted rights to the object.

A STAROS object contains two parts, a *data portion* and a *capability portion* (or C-list). The portions are stored in a single contiguous memory segment. Objects cannot grow dynamically and therefore retain the size with which they were created. The data portion is located at the low-address end of the segment, and the capability portion is located at the high-address end. A process possessing a suitably privileged object capability can directly manipulate the data portion of the object with processor data instructions.

A STAROS process can directly address 64K bytes of memory (local or remote) at any time. This limit is dictated by the 16-bit PDP-11 addressing architecture. STAROS partitions this address space into 16 4K-byte windows. Each STAROS object has a maximum size of 4K bytes in its data portion and 256 slots in its capability portion. A suitably privileged process can request that an object's data portion be mapped into one of its windows, allowing direct instruction access.

The STAROS kernel defines a small set of object types, as listed in Table 7-1. These are known as *representation types*, and

BASIC OBJECT	Segment with data portion and C-list.
C-LIST	Basic object with capability portion only.
PROCESS OBJECT	Schedulable entity that contains the root C-list for addressing.
STACK OBJECT	An object supporting PUSH and POP stack operations.
DEQUE OBJECT	A two-ended stack, supporting PUSH and POP at head and tail.
DIRECTORY OBJECT	An object containing descriptors of physical object information.
DATA MAILBOX	An object for sending and receiving data messages.
CAPABILITY MAILBOX	An object for sending and receiving capability messages.
DEVICE OBJECT	The representation of a physical I/O device.

Table 7-1: STAROS Representation Types

instances of these types are known as *representation objects*. Operations on representation objects are supported by calls to StarOS. All other objects are implemented by user-defined type managers that construct other abstractions out of the basic representation objects. These user-defined types are known as *abstract types* and their instances are called *abstract objects*. Thus, an abstract object has an abstract type, which indicates the operations that can be performed on the object, and a representation type, which indicates the kernel type from which that object is constructed.

7.3 StarOS Capabilities

All references to StarOS objects, representation or abstract, are made through capabilities. A StarOS capability is 32-bits long and contains a 3-bit type field, a 13-bit rights field, and a 16-bit data word field, as illustrated in Figure 7-2. The interpretation of the data word depends on the capability type. StarOS supports several capability types, and the capability type field specifies one of the types listed in Table 7-2. The data capability is used to transmit small amounts (16 bits) of information efficiently without requiring the creation of a basic object and its overhead. The representation and abstract capabilities contain unique 16-bit names in their data words. A type manager token capability contains a unique 16-bit type identifier in its data word, allowing the possessor to operate on abstract objects of that type.

The capability rights field consists of several type-dependent and type-independent fields, as illustrated in Figure 7-2.

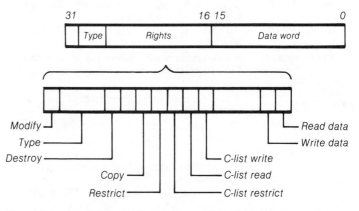

Figure 7-2: StarOS Capability and Capability Rights Word

REPRESENTATION CAPABILITY
>Names one of the kernel-defined representation objects and contains kernel-interpreted rights to the object.

ABSTRACT CAPABILITY
>Names an abstract object and contains type-specific rights.

TOKEN CAPABILITY
>Identifies the owner as the possessor of a special privilege (for example, as the garbage collection process or as the type manager for a specific type).

NULL CAPABILITY Marks an empty slot in an object's capability part.

DATA CAPABILITY Contains a 16-bit data value in its data word.

Table 7-2: STAROS Capability Types

Bits 0-7 of the rights word contain rights to the object addressed by the capability. For an abstract capability, this 8-bit field is defined and interpreted by the type manager. The rights shown in Figure 7-2 are for a representation capability for a basic object. Basic object rights permit reading and writing of the data part, loading and storing of capabilities in the C-list, and restriction of capability rights in the C-list of the object to which the capability points.

The *copy* and *restrict* rights apply to the capability itself and indicate whether or not the capability can be copied or if rights in it can be restricted. A capability without restrict rights can never be deleted, so new copies of capabilities are always given restrict rights. Finally, the *modify* and *destroy* rights are generic object rights, and specify whether the addressed object can be destroyed or modified in any way. Modify rights operate as in Hydra—modification of an object requires modify rights in each capability along the path to the target object.

7.4 Object Addressing

Each representation object or abstract object is addressed through a capability that contains its 16-bit unique name. At any time there can be many capabilities for an object, but there is only one 16-byte *descriptor* for each object. The *descriptor*, which corresponds to a Hydra active fixed part, is located on the cluster on which the object is stored. The format of an object descriptor is shown in Figure 7-3.

The garbage collection process uses the color field to indi-

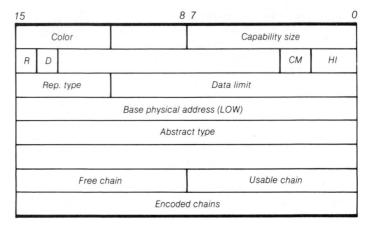

Figure 7-3: STAROS Object Descriptor Format

cate the garbage collection status of the object (for example, whether a capability for the object has been passed outside the local cluster). The capability size and data limit fields specify the size of the capability portion (in slots) and data portion (in bytes) of the object. Since the object is stored contiguously, these fields determine the total size of the object and the position of the dividing line between data and capability portions.

The object's primary memory location is formed by concatenating the base physical address field with the 2-bit HI field. This 18-bit address is local to the cluster processor specified by the computer module number (CM). An object must be stored on the same cluster as its descriptor, although capabilities for an object can be passed outside the cluster. Two type fields contain the abstract type of the object and the representation type used to implement it. Finally, the chain fields are used to form linked lists of descriptors, and R and D are reference and dirty bits, respectively.

Descriptors are stored in *directories*. Each CM⋆ cluster can have up to 32 directories, each containing up to 256 descriptors. A single *root directory* in each cluster contains descriptors for itself and the 31 subdirectories. STAROS 16-bit object names, contained in both abstract and representation capabilities, directly locate an object descriptor in one of these directories. A unique name specifies a 3-bit cluster number, a 5-bit directory number, and an 8-bit directory index, as shown in Figure 7-4.

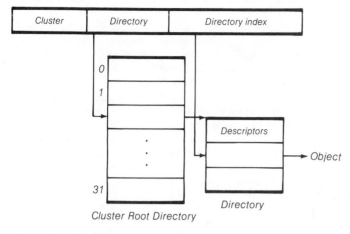

Figure 7-4: STAROS Directory Structure

7.5 STAROS Abstract Type Management

As previously stated, a type manager creates each new abstract object from one representation object (usually a basic object). The type manager returns an abstract capability for a new abstract object to a caller, but only the type manager can operate directly on the representation object implementing the abstraction. The possessor of an abstract capability can only use it as a parameter in a call to the type manager to request an object operation.

The key to a type manager's special ability is its *type token*, one of the capabilities previously described. Every type manager possesses a type token whose data word contains a unique identifier for its type. The type token is never given out except to procedures that are part of the type manager. The type manager uses the type token in the following way:

- When a process wishes to create a new abstract object, it calls the appropriate type manager. The type manager, through a call to STAROS, creates a new representation object, for which it receives a fully-privileged representation capability. The type manager then uses this capability to initialize the object as needed.

- After the object has been initialized, the type manager executes an ASSOCIATE TYPE instruction, specifying the object's representation capability and the manager's type token as parameters. This instruction stores the abstract type field from the token into the object's descriptor. The ASSOCIATE

133

TYPE instruction thus creates an *abstract object* from a *representation object*.

- Next, the type manager executes a DEAMPLIFY instruction to transform its fully-privileged representation capability into an abstract capability. The DEAMPLIFY instruction simply changes the type field in the capability from "representation" to "abstract."
- The type manager then returns the abstract capability to the caller. This abstract capability identifies the holder as having authority to request operations on that object. It cannot be used to access the encapsulated representation object directly.
- To perform an operation on the object, the holder of the abstract capability calls a type manager procedure, passing the abstract capability as a parameter. The type manager then executes an AMPLIFY instruction, specifying as operands the abstract capability and the type manager's private type token. If the type token's type matches the object's abstract type, the AMPLIFY instruction turns the abstract capability back into a fully-privileged representation capability, allowing the type manager to access the representation object.

7.6 Discussion

It is interesting to note the ways in which StarOS differs from the Hydra object model. StarOS limits direct access of an object's representation to the type manager. Two basic types of capabilities are provided: representation capabilities used to access kernel types, and abstract capabilities passed to users of type manager implemented objects. By turning a representation capability into an abstract capability, the type manager *seals* the capability with its special type token. Although the abstract capability has the object ID sealed within it, it cannot be used to access the object's representation. The type token is the key used later to *unseal* the capability, returning a representation capability that can manipulate the object. In this way, the type manager always receives full privilege to access any of the objects whose representation it controls.

Type tokens are a simplification of the Hydra amplification template. Hydra permitted more precise control of object access; an amplification template could be used to amplify only those rights needed by the type management procedure. In contrast, the StarOS type token mechanism always gives the type manager complete access to one of its objects.

The type token is thus a special type of capability used to seal or unseal another capability. Tokens are also used to identify specially privileged processes. Because tokens are capabilities, they are stored in C-lists and therefore cannot be fabricated by users. The data capability provides an efficient means for transmitting or sharing one word of information without creating a single-word object. Data capabilities also allow small amounts of data to be sent to a capability mailbox.

Another interesting feature of STAROS is its return to a small object address space. An object's unique ID, 16 bits in length, can be used to directly locate the descriptor for an object, thus simplifying the manipulation of capabilities and objects. The structure of the ID implies that the system can support a maximum of 8K objects per cluster on each of 8 clusters. The ID leads directly to a particular cluster. Of course, this scheme makes it difficult to move an object from one cluster to another because the address is not location independent. Indeed, objects are never relocated in this way.

Finally, the implementation of operating system functions in Kmap microcode had significant performance impact. For example, a standard capability operation on STAROS takes 100 microseconds, while a similar operation on Hydra takes 1 millisecond. The ability to access an object's data portion directly is more significant. Once an object is mapped through an addressing window (at a cost of about 70 microseconds), data words can be accessed directly in several microseconds. The Hydra overhead for copying data from and to the object data-part is a millisecond.

7.7 For Further Reading

A more detailed description of STAROS is provided in [Gehringer 81], and a description of CM* switching structure and addressing can be found in [Swan 78]. The STAROS task force concept is presented in [Jones 78b]. Performance measurements for STAROS (in comparison with Medusa, a second operating system developed on CM*) can be found in [Jones 80a], which also discusses CM* and some of its applications.

The IBM System/38 computer. (Courtesy International Business Machines.)

The IBM System/38

8.1 Introduction

IBM's capability-based System/38 [Berstis 80a, Houdek 81, IBM 8a, IBM 82b], announced in 1978 and delivered in 1980, is an outgrowth of work that began in the late sixties and early seventies on IBM's future system (FS) project. Designers at the IBM Development Laboratory in Rochester, Minnesota incorporated ideas from FS, modified by their needs, to produce a system for the commercial marketplace. It is interesting that such an advanced, object-based architecture has been applied to a very traditional product space. Initially, only the COBOL and RPG III languages were provided. The system, which includes the CPF (Control Program Facility) operating system, is intended to support transaction processing and database applications constructed in commercial languages.

A major goal of the System/38 design is to maintain programmer independence from the system implementation [Dahlby 80]; IBM wished to retain maximum flexibility to modify System/38's implementation for future technologies while supporting previously written System/38 programs. The designers also wished to support a high level of integrity and security at the machine interface and to support commonly executed user and system functions efficiently, such as database searches and memory management [Hoffman 80]. To meet these goals, IBM chose a layered machine structure with a high-level programming interface. The layers of this design are shown in Figure 8-1.

At the lowest level is a hardware machine that directly exe-

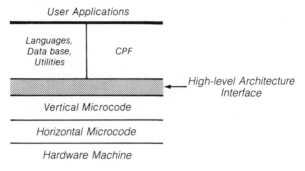

Figure 8-1: System/38 Implementation Layers

cutes 32-bit *horizontal* microcode. This horizontal microcode implements a more-or-less standard 32-bit register machine that executes *vertical* microcode.[1] The interface above the vertical microcode, called the high-level architecture interface in Figure 8-1, is the level described in this chapter; it supports the user-visible (or CPF-visible) System/38.

This high-level architecture interface is supported across implementations, while the structure of the underlying layers can change. For example, performance-critical functions, such as interprocess communication and memory allocation, are handled by the horizontal microcode. The system object and capability support is handled in part by both microcode layers. Different functions can be moved between microcode levels or into hardware in future versions, as performance experience is gained. In fact, this movement has already occurred on newer System/38 releases and models.

The CPF operating system and the vertical microcode are implemented in PL/S, a PL/I-like system programming language. There are approximately 900,000 lines of high-level PL/S code and an additional 400,000 lines of microcode support needed to implement CPF and its program products. The System/38 hardware includes a non-removable disk that holds this large store of microcode.

The System/38's high-level architecture interface is actually an *intermediate language* produced by all System/38 compilers. Before a program is executed, CPF translates this intermediate language into vertical microcode and calls to vertical microcode

---

[1]Although IBM calls this layer vertical microcode, it would generally not be considered microcode because it resembles a traditional IBM 370-like 32-bit instruction set and is programmed in a high-level language.

procedures. That is, the high-level interface is not directly executed. This translation process is described later.

IBM terminology is used throughout this chapter for compatibility with System/38 publications; it differs somewhat from that used in previous chapters. In particular, IBM uses the following terms: *space* for segment, *pointer* for capability, *authority* for rights, and *context* for directory. These synonyms will be presented again as each of the terms is introduced.

8.2 System Objects

System/38 instructions operate on two types of entities: *scalar data elements* and *system objects*. The scalar types are 16- and 32-bit signed binary, zoned and packed decimal, and character strings. The machine supports 14 types of system objects, described in Table 8-1. A set of type-specific instructions is provided for each system type.

SPACE	byte-addressable storage segment
PROGRAM	procedure instructions and associated data
USER PROFILE	object containing information about user's resource limits and authority to access any system objects
CONTEXT	directory of object names and capabilities
QUEUE	message queue for interprocess communication
DATA SPACE	collection of identically-structured records
DATA SPACE INDEX	object used to provide logical ordering for data space entries
CURSOR	direct interface to entries in a data space, or indirect interface through a data space index
INDEX	accesses data sequences based on key values
PROCESS CONTROL SPACE	object containing state information for a process
ACCESS GROUP	set of objects grouped together for paging performance reasons
LOGICAL UNIT DESCRIPTION	object describing an I/O device
CONTROLLER DESCRIPTION	object describing the attributes of a device controller
NETWORK DESCRIPTION	object describing a communications port

Table 8-1: System/38 System Object Types

Each system object consists of two parts: a functional portion and an optional space portion, as shown in Figure 8-2. The *functional portion* of an object is a segment containing object state (its representation); the data in the functional portion can be examined and modified only by microcode as a result of type-specific instructions. Thus, the functional portion is said to be *encapsulated* because it is not accessible to programs [Pinnow 80]. Optionally, a *space portion* can be associated with an object (IBM uses the word *space* to refer to a storage segment). The space portion is an attached segment for storing scalars and pointers that can be directly manipulated by user programs.

Every object in the system has several associated attributes. First is a *type* that identifies it as one of the 14 system object types listed in Table 8-1. (Objects can also have *subtypes* for further software classification.) Second is a symbolic *text name* chosen by the user to refer to the object. Last is a *unique identifier* (ID) that uniquely specifies an object for the life of the system. Object identifiers are never reused. When an object is created, the object ID is assigned by the system, while the text name and type are specified by the programmer.

Although the contents and format of the encapsulated data in an object are not programmer accessible, programmers must be able to specify initial object values or examine an object's state. The System/38 instruction set uses templates to convey initial information and communicate encapsulated data. A template is simply a data structure with defined fields used to transmit information at the instruction level. For example, the CREATE QUEUE instruction needs to specify some information about the maximum number of messages, the size of messages, the queueing discipline, and so on. This information is

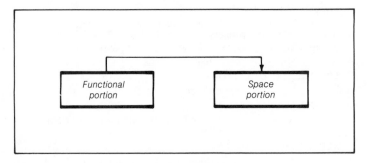

Figure 8-2: IBM System/38 System Object

conveyed by creating a template in a space and specifying a
capability to that space as a parameter to the instruction.
Later, an instruction can be executed to produce a template
showing information about the queue. Although the architecture fixes the format of the template used to communicate information at the high-level interface, it does not dictate how
that information is maintained once it is encapsulated within
the object.

The only object not containing a functional part is a *space
object*. A space object is a contiguous segment and is the only
object that can be manipulated at the byte level by scalar
instructions.

A system object, then, is an instance of an abstract data
type. System/38 instructions exist to create, manipulate, examine, and delete each of the system object types. The machine
provides an interface that hides the implementation of an object from the user. An object's state is stored in one or more
segments; its attributes include a type that indicates what operations are allowed and an identifier that uniquely specifies the
object. A base segment for each object contains pointers to any
other segments composing the object, as well as type and ID
information.

8.3 Object Addressing

Before examining object addressing in detail, it is necessary
to describe memory management and segment addressing on
the System/38. Object addressing, using capabilities, is based
on lower-level segment addressing mechanisms.

8.3.1 Virtual Memory

The IBM System/38 architecture supports a flat, single-
level, 64-bit virtual address space. To the user at the high-level
interface (either the operating system or application programmer), all addressable objects and segments are in directly accessible memory; there is no concept of secondary storage. The
System/38 microcode is responsible for moving segments between primary and secondary storage to create this virtual
memory environment.

The structure of a 64-bit virtual address is shown in Figure
8-3. The System/38 segment size is 64K bytes. Each segment is
divided into 512-byte pages. The low-order 16 bits of the ad-

16	24	8	7	9
Microcode extended	Segment identification	Group ID	Page number	Byte offset

Figure 8-3: System/38 Virtual Address

dress thus provide the page number and byte offset for the pages of a segment. For larger objects, up to 256 segments can be grouped together into segment groups. The group ID field specifies which 64K-byte segment is being addressed within a 16M-byte segment group. The next 24 bits of the address provide a unique segment ID for the segment group.

The System/38 hardware only supports 48-bit physical addresses composed of these fields. However, when an object is created, the microcode extends the address to 64 bits by adding an additional 16-bit field.

The full 64-bit address is stored in a special header with the segment. When a 64-bit address is used to access a segment, the upper 16 bits of the address are compared with the upper 16 bits of address in the segment's header. If a mismatch occurs, the addressed object has been destroyed and the reference is not allowed. At any one time, then, there can only be 2^{24} or 16 million segment groups in existence.

Because the address space is so large, particularly with the 16-bit extension to the segment ID field, segment IDs are never reused. The system assigns a new segment ID at creation that is unique for the life of the system. If the object is deleted, references to the segment ID are not allowed. The system need not search for dangling references when an object is deleted. The segment ID, therefore, provides a mechanism for determining the unique ID for system objects. System objects are named with the unique ID of the first segment containing the functional portion of the object. The unique ID is the upper six bytes of the virtual address.

8.3.2 Pointers

As in other capability systems, objects as well as scalar data elements are addressed through capabilities. System/38 capabilities are known as *pointers*. There are four types of pointers in the System/38:

- *system pointers* address the 14 system object types (listed in Table 8-1),
- *space pointers* address a specific byte within a space object (segment),
- *data pointers* address a specific byte within a space and also contain attribute information describing the type of element (e.g., character or decimal), and
- *instruction pointers* address branch targets within programs.

Each System/38 pointer is 16 bytes long. In order to access an object or an element within a segment, a program must specify a pointer that addresses the object or segment element. Pointers can contain different information at various times, including symbolic text names, authorization information (access rights), the object type, and the unique ID for system pointers or virtual address for data and space pointers. The information within a pointer can be modified, for example, from text name to unique ID, to allow for late binding of the pointer to the object.

Unlike the systems previously examined, which use C-lists for the storage of capabilities, System/38 pointers can be freely mixed in segments along with scalar data. To allow storing of capabilities with data in the same segment while still maintaining capability integrity, the System/38 implements a memory tagging scheme. Memory is byte addressable and words are 32 bits long. However, physical words of primary memory are actually 40 bits wide. Invisible to the programmer are a 1-bit tag field and a 7-bit error correcting code. Pointers must be aligned on 16-byte boundaries. When a pointer is stored in a segment by a valid pointer instruction, the hardware sets the associated tag bits for the four consecutive 32-bit words used to hold the pointer. Any instruction that requires a pointer operand checks that the pointer is aligned and that the four tag bits are set before using the element for addressing. Program data instructions can freely examine pointers. However, if a program instruction modifies any data in a pointer, the microcode turns off the tag bit in the associated word or words, invalidating the pointer.

Table 8-2 lists some of the instructions that operate on System/38 pointers. Note that a space object (a memory segment) is a system *object* that is addressed by a system *pointer*. A space pointer, on the other hand, is a capability that addresses a particular byte in a space object.

ADD SPACE POINTER

adds a signed offset to the byte address in a space pointer

COMPARE POINTER FOR ADDRESSABILITY

compares two pointers to see if they address the same object, the same space, or the same space element

RESOLVE POINTER searches a directory (see Section 8.3.3) for a named object and returns a pointer for that object

SET DATA POINTER

returns a data pointer for an element in a space

SET SPACE POINTER

returns a space pointer for an element in a space

SET SPACE POINTER FROM POINTER

if the source is a space or data pointer, creates a space pointer for the specified byte; or if the source is a system pointer, returns a space pointer for the associated space

SET SYSTEM POINTER FROM POINTER

if the source is a space or data pointer, returns a pointer for the system object containing the associated space; if the source is a system pointer, returns a system pointer for that same object

Table 8-2:   System/38 Pointer Instructions

8.3.3 Contexts

Pointers are used to address objects; however, users refer to objects by symbolic text names. System objects called *contexts* implement directories for storing symbolic object names and pointers. When a new object is created, its symbolic name and an associated pointer are stored in a specified context. Table 8-3 lists the context instructions supported by the System/38.

The symbolic names stored in contexts are not necessarily unique, and a user can possess several contexts containing the same name but referring to different objects. This feature allows for testing and logical object substitution. A program that refers to an object by name can receive different objects depending on what context is used for name resolution. When a reference is made to a pointer containing an object name, the system examines the user's *Name Resolution List* (NRL). The NRL contains pointers to user contexts in the order that they should be searched. By changing the context ordering or manipulating entries, the user can change the objects on which the program operates.

CREATE CONTEXT	creates a new context object and returns a system pointer to address it
DESTROY CONTEXT	deletes a context object
MATERIALIZE CONTEXT	returns name and pointer for one or more objects addressed by a context
RENAME OBJECT	changes the symbolic name for an object in a context

Table 8-3: System/38 Context Instructions

8.3.4 Physical Address Mapping

Because of the large size of a System/38 virtual address, standard address translation schemes involving indexing of segment/page tables with the segment/page number address field cannot be used. Instead, the System/38 hardware uses hashing with linked list collision resolution to find the primary memory address for a specified virtual address.

The basic units of physical and virtual storage are 512-byte pages. A translation scheme is used to locate a page in primary memory. The upper 39 bits of a 48-bit virtual address, encompassing the unique segment ID, specify a unique virtual page address for the page. A hashing function is applied to these bits to obtain an index into a data structure called the *Hash Index Table* (HIT), shown in Figure 8-4. The hashing function is an EXCLUSIVE-OR of low-order bits from the segment ID and group ID fields, and reverse-order bits from the page number field. This function provides uniform mapping from the sparse address space to the HIT [Houdek 80].

The HIT entry contains an index of an entry in the *Page Directory Table* (PDT). The PDT contains one entry for each page of primary memory. Each entry contains the virtual address of a corresponding primary memory page. That is, the index into the PDT is the page frame number for the virtual address described in the entry. Each entry also contains a link. The hardware checks the virtual address at the first entry pointed to by the HIT and follows the linked list until a virtual address match is found or the list ends. If a match is found, the index of that entry is used as the page frame number in the primary memory address. If no match is found, the page is not

145

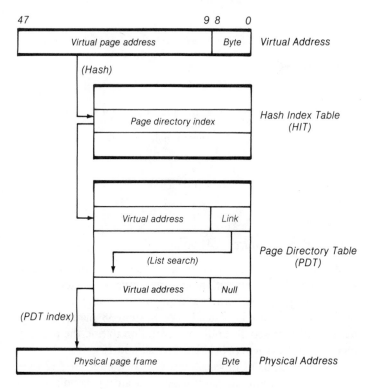

Figure 8-4: System/38 Virtual Address Translation

in primary memory and the hardware must load the page from secondary storage.

The performance of this search depends on the uniformity of the hashing function and the length of the lists in the Page Directory Table. In order to shorten the list lengths, the Hash Index Table is constructed to be twice the size of the Page Directory Table.

Two optimizations are used to avoid this two-level table search on every reference. First, the hardware contains a two-way associative translation buffer to cache recent address translations (the buffer size is different for different System/38 models, typically 2 x 64 or 2 x 128 entries). To check the translation buffer, the virtual page field is hashed to an offset that selects one entry in each half of the buffer. The two selected entries, which contain a virtual page address and translated primary memory page frame number, are checked for a match. If the virtual address matches, the page frame number is used to construct the primary memory address. If no match occurs, the table search proceeds, eventually replacing one of the selected translation buffer entries with its data, based on a least recently used bit.

The second optimization is the use of *resolved address registers* in the hardware. These registers are used in the CPU to hold virtual page, physical page, and byte offset information while a page is being processed. As long as references are made to the addressed page (e.g., during the sequential search of elements of an array), the hardware need not search the translation buffer for consecutive accesses.

8.4 Profiles and Authority

The System/38 hardware provides a mechanism for ensuring privacy and separation of data and for sharing information between users. The basic unit of computation, from which protection stems, is the *process*. Each user process is defined by a *Process Control Space* object that contains its state. When a user logs onto the system, a new process is created; a *user profile* object is associated with that process based on the user's name. The user profile contains:

- the user's name,
- the user's password,
- any special authorization or privileges the user possesses,
- the maximum priority,
- the maximum storage usage,
- an initial program to run upon log-in (if any),
- a list of objects that the user owns, and
- a list of non-owned objects that the user is authorized to access, and the permitted authorities.

All authority to perform operations on objects is rooted in the user profile. When an object is created, it is created with an attribute stating whether the object is permanent or temporary. The profile associated with the process issuing the CREATE operation on a permanent object becomes the owner of the object. An owner has all rights to the object and can perform any operations, including deletion. Temporary objects receive no protection and have no owner. They are destroyed when the system is booted.

The owner of an object can grant various types of access to other user profiles in the system. There are a number of *authorities,* or access rights, that a process can have with respect to an object. The authorities define what object operations the

147

process can perform. The authorities also define what operations can be performed on pointers for the object. Object authorities are divided into three categories:

- *object control* authority gives the possessor control of the object's existence (for example, the right to delete or transfer ownership),
- *object management* authority permits the holder to change addressability (for example, to rename the object or grant authority to other profiles), and
- *operational management* authority includes basic access rights to the contents of the object, such as retrieve, insert, delete, and update entry privilege.

The authority information for each object is thus profile-based. Each user has a profile that indicates what objects are owned and what access is permitted to other objects. If a user wishes to allow access for an owned object to another user, the owner *grants* authority for the object to the sharer's profile. To execute a GRANT AUTHORITY instruction, a user must own an object or have object management rights. A user cannot grant an authority that the user does not possess.

Table 8-4 lists some of the profile/authority management instructions supported by the System/38. These instructions allow a properly authorized user to grant access privileges to other users, to examine what objects are authorized to him or her, and to see what authorizations have been given to other users for owned objects.

In addition to specific object authority granted to specific profiles, each object can have an associated *public authorization*. The object's owner grants public authority with the GRANT AUTHORITY instruction by omitting the profile parameter. The public authority is stored in the object's header and allows any user to access the object in the permitted modes. When an attempt is made to access an object, the public authority is checked first. If the access is not permitted by the object's public authority, the user's profile is then examined.

8.4.1 Authority/Pointer Resolution

Thus far, the System/38 protection mechanism has been described from the perspective of the profile object. The profile provides a standard *Access Control List* mechanism. The owner of an object can explicitly permit other profiles to have access to that object and can later *revoke* that access.

CREATE USER PROFILE
 builds a new user profile (this operation is privileged)

DESTROY USER PROFILE
 deletes a profile

GRANT AUTHORITY
 grants specified authorities for an object to a specified user profile

MATERIALIZE AUTHORIZED OBJECTS
 returns list of all owned objects or authorized objects

MATERIALIZE AUTHORIZED USERS
 returns a list of owning or authorized users for a specified object

RETRACT AUTHORITY
 revokes or modifies authority for an object from a specified user profile

TEST AUTHORITY   tests if specified authorities are granted to the current process for a specified object

TRANSFER OWNERSHIP
 transfers ownership of an object to another profile

Table 8-4:   System/38 Authority Management Instructions

The ability to revoke object access is an important part of the System/38 design; this feature has not been provided in any of the previously examined systems. Revocation is, in fact, a difficult problem in capability systems and is generally expensive to implement in terms of addressing overhead. The IBM System/38 design allows an object's owner to decide whether revocation is needed for the object. The System/38 provides two pointer formats: one for which access can be revoked and another for which access cannot be revoked. An object's owner can decide which type of pointer to use for each object in each instance depending on the relative importance of revocation and addressing efficiency.

In order to access an object in the System/38 a process must possess a pointer for that object. Pointers can be stored in two formats: *unauthorized* and *authorized*. An unauthorized pointer contains an object's unique identifier but *does not* contain authorizations (i.e., access rights) to the object. When an unauthorized pointer is used to access an object, the hardware checks the profile of the executing process to verify that the requested operation is permitted. Without this check, revoca-

149

tion of authority would be impossible. An unauthorized pointer, then, cannot be used in the way that traditional capabilities can be used. Additional overhead is added to pointer usage because of the profile check.

In cases where revocation is not required or higher performance is needed, access rights can be stored in a pointer, creating an *authorized pointer*. An authorized pointer acts as a capability, and reference to an object with an authorized pointer does not require a profile lookup. The RESOLVE SYSTEM POINTER instruction is used to create authorized pointers. An authorized pointer can only be created by a user whose profile has object management authority for the object; the created pointer cannot have rights not available to the creating profile. Once constructed, an authorized pointer maintains authority to access an object for the life of that object. The pointer can be stored and passed to other processes. Because the profile check is avoided with authorized pointer usage, authority cannot be revoked later.

8.5 Programs/Procedures

IBM uses the term *program* to refer to what is typically called a procedure or subroutine. A System/38 program is an executable system object. A program object is created by a CREATE PROGRAM instruction, which specifies a template containing System/38 instructions and associated data structures. The CREATE PROGRAM instruction returns a system pointer allowing the program to be called.

As noted previously, the System/38 source language (i.e., the high-level architecture interface shown in Figure 8-1) is really an intermediate language produced by compilers. The effect of the CREATE PROGRAM instruction is to compile this intermediate language source into microcode that can be executed on the next lowest "level" of the machine. Source instructions, depending on their complexity, either compile directly into System/38 vertical micro-instructions or into micro-procedure calls. The compiled program is thus encapsulated in the program object, and the form of the micro-machine is hidden by the CREATE PROGRAM instruction. Once encapsulated, the format of a program object cannot be examined.

Thus, the System/38 high-level architecture is *never directly executed*. It is a specification for a language that all System/38 implementations support; however, that language is translated into a proprietary vertical micro-language before execution. The format of the encapsulated program in this micro-language cannot be examined and can be different on different System/38 implementations.

8.5.1 The Instruction Stream

The program template presented to the CREATE PROGRAM instruction consists of three parts:

- a program consisting of a sequence of instructions,
- an *Object Definition Table* (ODT), and
- user data.

Each instruction consists of a number of 2-byte fields including an operation code, an optional operation code extender, and one to four operands. The operands can specify literals, elements in space objects, pointers to system objects, and so on. The information about operand addressing and characteristics is stored in the Object Definition Table included in the template. The ODT is a dictionary that describes operands for the instruction stream.

Each instruction operand contains an index into the Object Definition Table. The ODT actually consists of two parts: a vector of fixed-length (4-byte) elements called the *Object Directory Vector* (ODV), and a vector of variable-length entries called the *ODT Entry String* (OES). An operand is either completely described by its 4-byte ODV entry, or the ODV entry has a partial description and a pointer into the OES, where the remaining description is found. Most commonly occurring cases are handled by the fixed-length ODV itself. Several ODV entries can point to the same OES entry. The ODT can contain information such as operand type (e.g., fixed-length decimal string), size, location, allocation (static or dynamic), initial value, and so on. Figure 8-5 shows an example of an instruction with three operands. The operands index ODT information defining their type and location.

Each instruction operand consists of one or more 2-byte fields. The first 2-byte field contains a 3-bit mode field and a 13-bit ODV index. The mode field indicates what type of addressing is required and what additional 2-byte fields (called secondary operands) follow in the instruction stream to describe the operand completely. For example, a string operand may require three 2-byte fields to describe a base, index, and length.

151

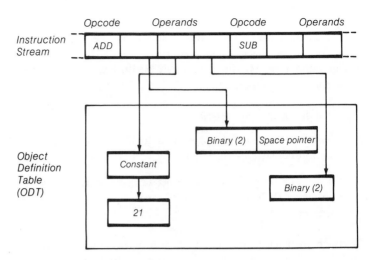

Figure 8-5: System/38 Example High-level Instruction

Since the ODT completely describes each operand, the scalar opcodes are generic. For example, there is only one ADD NUMERIC instruction that operates on all numeric data types. The machine interprets the ODT entry to decide how the operation should be performed and what conversions are required.

The *Object Mapping Table* (OMT) is the final data structure that is part of the encapsulated program (although not included in the initial template). It contains 6-byte mapping entries for each entry in the ODV that maps to a space.

8.5.2 Program Activation and Invocation

A program, then, is a system object that represents a separately compiled unit of execution (typically known as a procedure). Programs are called by the CALL instruction. There are actually two parts to the initiation of a program on the System/38: activation and invocation.

Before a program can be invoked (called), it must be *activated*. Activation of the program causes static storage for the program to be allocated and initialized. Also, any global variables in program static storage are made addressable. A process data structure called the *Process Static Storage Area* (PSSA) contains an activation entry for each activated program in the process. The activation entry contains status information, a count of the number of invocations using the activation, the size of static storage, and the storage itself. The first entry in the PSSA contains headers for the chain of activation entries and a free space chain.

Invocation occurs as the result of a transfer of control to the program. At invocation time, program automatic (that is, dynamic) storage is allocated and initialized in a process data structure called the *Process Automatic Storage Area* (PASA). Each invocation entry contains status information, a pointer to the previous invocation entry, a pointer to the program, and the automatic storage. After the invocation entry is allocated and initialized, control is transferred to the program at its entry point.

Activation can occur implicitly or explicitly. If invocation is requested of a program that has not been activated, activation is done automatically by the hardware.

8.5.3 Protected Procedures

The IBM System/38 provides a mechanism for creating protected subsystems. As on previous systems, a protected subsystem mechanism must allow programs to execute in an amplified protection environment. That is, some programs must be able to access objects not available to their caller. Since the System/38 profile object defines a domain of protection, protected subsystems are provided through profile-based facilities called *profile adoption* and *profile propagation*.

The authority of each System/38 process is determined by its profile. When a process calls a program, that program generally gains access to the process's profile and, therefore, to the process' objects. However, it is possible to construct System/38 programs that can access additional objects not available to the caller. When a program is created, the program's owner can specify that the program retain access to the *owner's* profile, as well as its caller's profile. This feature, called profile adoption, allows a called program to access objects not available to the caller and can be used to construct a protected subsystem.

Although the general calling mechanism allows a called program access to its caller's profile, a calling process can also restrict this ability. When a program is created, the program's owner can specify whether its profile should be *propagated* to programs on calls. Thus, a program can also see that its owner's profile is protected from access by programs further down the call chain.

153

8.6 Special Privileges

It is worth noting that there are some special privileges in the System/38 authorization system. In addition to object-based authorities stored in a user profile, there may be other permitted authorities that are not connected with any particular object. For example, the ability to create user profiles, diagnose the hardware, or create objects representing physical I/O devices can be controlled by authorizations in a user profile. Also, the ability to dump and load objects to removable storage is protected, as well as the ability to execute operations to modify or service system hardware attributes. Finally, some objects, such as user profiles and device descriptions, receive special protection and can only be addressed through a special machine context (directory).

8.7 Discussion

The IBM System/38 is a complex architecture constructed from several levels of hardware, microcode, and software. Because of its commercial orientation and the fact that it is available from IBM, the System/38 is probably destined to become, at least in the immediate future, the most pervasive object architecture.

The most interesting feature of the System/38, from the viewpoint of capability systems, is its use of tagging. Capabilities and data can be freely mixed in segments with no loss of integrity. The ability to mix data and capabilities generally permits more natural data structuring than the C-list approach. A single tag bit associated with each 32-bit word indicates whether or not the word is *part* of a capability. This tag bit is hidden from the programmer and accessible only to the microcode. To be used for addressing, a pointer must be aligned on a 16-byte boundary and have all four tag bits set. The alignment requirement prohibits the user from specifying four consecutive words with tags set that lie within two contiguous capabilities.

The integrity of a capability system must be ensured on secondary storage as well as in primary memory, and the pointer tags must be saved on secondary storage. On the System/38, each disk page is 520 bytes long and stores a 512-byte data page and an 8-byte header. The 8-byte header for each block contains the virtual address for the page, an indication of whether or not the page contains any pointers, and if so, which 16-byte quadword contains the first pointer in the page. Each page can contain, at most, 32 pointers; therefore, only 32 bits are required to specify whether each quadword contains a pointer. If a page contains pointers, the tag bits are stored within some unused bytes in the first 16-byte pointer on the page. When a page is written to disk, the hardware automatically writes the disk block header. When a page is read into primary memory, the header is automatically removed and the tags are reconstructed.

The System/38 architecture provides a large single-level address space. The details of memory management, I/O, and so on are hidden from the programmer. There is no need for a traditional file system. All objects can be declared permanent when created, can be stored for long periods of time, and can be addressed at any time as if they were in primary memory. Addressing is independent of the object's memory residency characteristics. One problem with schemes that remove the abstraction of secondary storage is in transaction systems or reliable data base operations. In some instances, the programmer may wish to ensure that the latest copy of a segment or object is checkpointed onto long-term storage. The one-level memory scheme has removed the ability to express the thought of writing the segment to disk. To solve this, CPF allows an object attribute that states how frequently data is to be backed up for a particular object.

The System 38 permits revocation by adding an access control list mechanism to the capability addressing mechanism. Two types of pointers, authorized and unauthorized, can be used depending on whether or not revocation is required. Authorized pointers are traditional capabilities because they contain access rights and can be freely copied. Passing an authorized pointer passes both the addressing rights and privileges. The ability to resolve a pointer to load the access rights is controlled by an authorized pointer authorization. Only suitably privileged profiles can create an authorized pointer.

In contrast, an unauthorized pointer is not a capability in the traditional sense. The same unauthorized pointer can permit different types of access when used by different processes. This is because the authorization rights are fetched from the process's profile when a reference is made. This extra step in pointer address evaluation permits explicit control over authority and combines the advantages of standard capability systems and access control lists. The user can specify (and determine at any time) what other profiles are allowed access to the user's objects. If only unauthorized pointers have been distributed, access can be revoked by removing authorization from other profiles.

Unauthorized pointers permit revocation but add complexity to the handling of pointers. For example, to pass a pointer to another process, the possessor of the pointer must be aware of whether that pointer is authorized or unauthorized. Unauthorized pointers, unlike capabilities, are not context independent. If the pointer is unauthorized, passing it to another process will not permit object access unless permission has been granted to the other process's profile. Also, unauthorized pointers cannot easily be used to build and share data structures. For example, if a user wishes to build a tree structure of segments and pass the tree or subtrees to other processes, the authorization scheme requires that authorization for each segment be granted separately to each profile involved.

The structuring of System/38 authorizations permits close control of pointers. Given the division of authority into object control, management, and access, it is possible for one user to be able to affect the propagation of addresses but not be able to access object data. Another user may be able to read and write but not propagate pointers.

The large size of the System/38 address space simplifies many problems. Segment identifiers are large enough that they are never reused. This allows use of the segment ID as a unique name for an object. Since the ID is never reused, there is no problem with dangling references. An attempt to access a deleted object simply causes an exception. Large IDs also simplify the implementation of the one-level memory system. There is no separation of long-term unique ID and address. The unique ID is the virtual address used to access a specific object, segment, or byte. There is no need for separate inform and outform capabilities or for transforming capabilities in memory when a segment is removed from memory.

Although the System/38 instruction stream and Object Definition Table are never used for direct execution, this interface has some interesting features. The ODT provides a form of tagging somewhat different from the tagged architectures examined earlier. Each data element is tagged; however, the tag is part of the operand, not part of the element. This allows for several different views of the same data element; different instructions can treat the same word as different data types. Operation codes can be generic, and conversion, truncation, etc. can be performed based on type information in the ODT. The information stored in the ODT and I-stream may not be extremely compact, but the program in this form need not be retained after a program object is created.

Finally, IBM has used the object programming approach to allow isolated construction of components of a very complex system. The object approach is intended to hide from the programmer the implementation details of the System/38 hardware, so that future System/38 implementations can take advantage of advances in technology without affecting existing programs. Although this has been a goal of other architectures, the System/38 has used the object approach to place the user/system boundary at an unusually high level, hiding many details of the machine. For example, the System/38 high-level architecture has no registers, although the vertical microcode is free to use registers or to use different numbers of registers in different implementations.

The initial System/38 product, with its limitation to commercial languages, does not stress the architecture. It will be interesting in future years to see if IBM approaches other markets with this object-based machine structure.

8.8 For Further Reading

Detailed information about the System/38 high-level architecture can be found in two IBM manuals [IBM 80a, IBM 82]. IBM has also packaged a collection of 30 short technical papers, mostly dealing with hardware and implementation issues, into a document called *IBM System/38 Technical Developments* [IBM 80b]. Several papers describing the addressing and protection features of System/38 have also been published in technical literature [Berstis 80a, Houdek 81, Soltis 79, Soltis 81].

The Intel iAXP 432 computer. (Courtesy Intel Corporation.)

The Intel iAPX 432

9.1 Introduction

In 1981, Intel introduced the first object-based microprocessor, the iAPX 432 [Intel 81, Rattner 81, Organick 83]. Like the IBM System/38, the Intel 432 implements many operating system functions in hardware and microcode, including process scheduling, interprocess communication, and storage allocation. The integration of such software operations in hardware is particularly impressive when considered with the Intel 432's VLSI implementation.

The Intel 432 design effort began in 1975 with an attempt to implement in silicon a system much like Carnegie-Mellon's Hydra operating system [Wulf 74a]. Three chips compose the Intel 432 processing elements. The central processing unit, called the General Data Processor (GDP), is implemented on two 64-pin VLSI chips. Together, the GDP chips contain over 160,000 components. The Interface Processor (IP), responsible for communication and data transfer between the Intel 432 and its I/O subsystems, is the third 64-pin chip. Design and layout of the chip set took more than 100 man-years.

The 432 is a multiprocessor system that can accommodate a total of six processors, each either a GDP or IP. The general structure of the 432 multiprocessor system is shown in Figure 9-1. All of the processors are connected to a single multiprocessor message bus through which they communicate with each other and with shared system memory. The IPs connect the multiprocessor system to Intel Multibus subsystems. Each Multibus is controlled by an associated processor, such as an

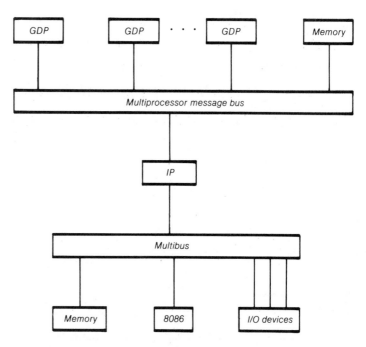

Figure 9-1: Intel iAPX 432 Structure

Intel 8086, that connects to local memory and some number of I/O devices. The IPs transfer data between Intel 432 memory and Multibus local memory; all I/O is actually performed by the associated processor.

The Intel 432 instruction set provides two types of instructions: scalar and object-oriented. The scalar instruction set consists of a small set of move and store operators, boolean arithmetic, binary and floating point arithmetic, and comparison operations. Scalar instructions operate on 8-bit characters, 16- and 32-bit signed and unsigned integers, and 32-, 64-, and 80-bit floating point numbers. The 432 has a stack architecture; instruction operands can be fetched from the stack and results can be pushed onto the stack. There are no general-purpose registers.

An object-oriented instruction set provides operations on abstract objects that are managed by a combination of hardware and software. The following sections examine many of those object types and the details of object addressing on the Intel 432. It should be noted that the Intel 432 architecture has evolved since its introduction; this chapter reflects the system as of revision 3 [Intel 82].

9.2 Segments and Objects

The concepts of object-based computing are deeply imbedded in the Intel 432. All system resources are represented as objects; for example, a *processor object* maintains the state of each GDP or IP in the system. Each processor object then contains a queue of *process objects*, which represent work to be scheduled and executed. All objects are addressed through capabilities which, on the Intel 432, are called access descriptors (ADs). (The vendor's terminology is used in this chapter for compatibility with Intel literature. The notation "AD" is used throughout for "capability.")

At the lowest level, objects are composed of memory segments, and a memory segment is the most fundamental object (called a *generic object* on the Intel 432). Each Intel 432 segment has two parts: a *data part* for scalars and an *access part* for ADs, as shown in Figure 9-2. Objects requiring both data and access descriptors can be stored in a single segment. Segments are addressed through ADs, as the figure illustrates. The data part grows upward (in the positive direction) from the boundary between the two parts, while the access part grows downward (in the negative direction) from the dividing line. The hardware ensures that only data operations are performed on the data part and that AD operations are performed on the access part.

Each part of a segment can be from 0 to 64K bytes in size. Data elements in the data part are addressed as byte displacements from the dividing line. ADs, which are 32-bits long, are addressed by integer indices from the dividing line. The access part can therefore contain up to 16K ADs. Both data elements and ADs are addressed as positive indices within the segment;

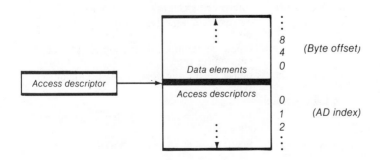

Figure 9-2: Intel 432 Segment

the hardware determines the part of the segment to access based on the type of the required operand.

In addition to basic storage segments, the Intel 432 hardware supports a number of system object types, listed in Table 9-1. The representation for an instance of a system object is maintained in a storage segment. Operating system type managers are responsible for creating new instances of system objects. A type manager creates and sets the type for an object through the CREATE TYPED OBJECT instruction. The operands for this instruction specify the object's type, the data part size, and the access part size. The instruction returns an AD for the new object, which the type manager uses to initialize the object appropriately.

For each system object type, the 432 architecture specifies the meaning of some of the data and/or access fields. These processor-defined fields are stored in the low-index portions of the two segment parts, adjacent to the boundary. A type manager is free to allocate additional data or access descriptor space in higher address parts of the two regions for object information needed by software.

GENERIC SEGMENT	basic storage for data and access descriptors (capabilities)
DYNAMIC SEGMENT	storage segment created by a programmer-defined type manager
INSTRUCTION SEGMENT	segment containing executable code
PROCESS	basic unit of scheduling
PROCESSOR	432 GDP or IP
DOMAIN	module or package
CONTEXT	dynamic state for a procedure invocation
MESSAGE PORT	interprocess communication object
CARRIER	extension of a message used to queue it to a port
TYPE DEFINITION	object containing information about a specific object type
TYPE CONTROL	object permitting creation of specific object types
STORAGE RESOURCE	source of primary memory for object storage allocation
OBJECT TABLE	mapping table of object descriptors

Table 9-1: Intel 432 System Object Types

As in previous capability-based systems, there are two components to the Intel 432 addressing structure. First, a single descriptor contains the physical mapping information for each object. These descriptors, on the Intel 432, are called *object descriptors*. Second, programs specify *access descriptors* to refer to objects that they wish to manipulate. All ADs for an object refer to that object indirectly through its single object descriptor. The following sections describe first object descriptors and then access descriptors.

9.3.1 Object Descriptors

For each Intel 432 object there is a single *object descriptor*. The object descriptor contains information about the physical location and state of the object. The purpose of the object descriptor is to locate this physical object information in a single place so that objects can be easily relocated or synchronized. Each object descriptor is 16 bytes long. There are several types of object descriptors, but the most common is a storage segment descriptor, shown in Figure 9-3. Table 9-2 describes the fields in the storage segment descriptor.

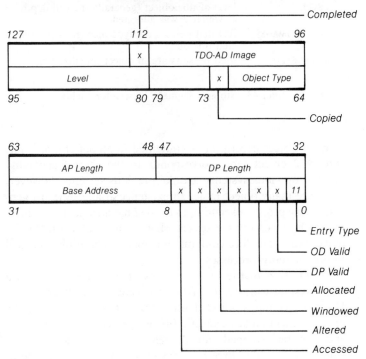

Figure 9-3: Intel 432 Storage Segments Descriptor   **163**

ENTRY TYPE	indicates that this is a storage descriptor
OD VALID	specifies whether the object descriptor can be used for addressing
DP VALID	indicates whether or not the object has a data part
ALLOCATED	specifies whether or not storage is allocated for this object
WINDOWED	indicates whether or not this object is being mapped by an IP
ALTERED	set to 1 whenever the object is written
ACCESSED	set to 1 whenever the object is accessed
BASE ADDRESS	primary memory address of the first byte of the segment's data part
DP LENGTH	length in bytes (minus one) of the segment's data part
AP LENGTH	length in bytes (minus one) of the segment's access part
OBJECT TYPE	type of the object, consisting of a 5-bit system type field (specifying system objects, shown in Table 9-1) and a 3-bit processor type field (specifying whether a GDP or IP owns the object)
COPIED	set to 1 whenever an AD referencing this object is copied
LEVEL	level of this object (generally the call depth at which it was allocated)
TDO-AD IMAGE	AD that defines the type manager that created this object
COMPLETED	used by software in object initialization

Table 9-2: Intel 432 Storage Segment Descriptor Fields

Each object descriptor is contained in an *object table.* The Intel 432 object table corresponds to the central capability table of previous systems. Unlike previous systems, however, there are many object tables in existence at any time. In general, every process executing in the 432 has an associated object table. Or, several processes can share a single object table. An object table therefore contains information about objects local to one or more processes.

In addition to the many process object tables, there is a *single* system-wide *Object Table Directory.* The Object Table Directory contains object descriptors that address each of the process object tables. Object tables are thus objects themselves and can be swapped out or relocated like other objects. The Object Table Directory, however, must always reside in primary memory. Each processor object contains the primary memory address of the Object Table Directory.

9.3.2 Access Descriptors

While each object has only one object descriptor, many *access descriptors* can be used to address the object. ADs are 32-bits long and specify addressing and access rights to an object. To execute an instruction that manipulates an object, the programmer specifies the location of an AD for the object. The AD is specified by its index in the access part of a segment. The collection of ADs accessible to a procedure define that procedure's execution environment: that is, the set of objects the procedure can address and manipulate.

An AD, illustrated in Figure 9-4, contains access rights to an object along with two 12-bit mapping indices. The read, write, and type rights fields are rights with respect to the addressed object. Type rights are type dependent and their encoding is different for each object type. Some type rights for system objects are defined by the architecture and evaluated by hardware instructions. The delete rights bit permits the possessor to delete the AD itself. An attempt to delete an AD with this bit set to zero causes a fault. The unchecked copy rights bit, indicating whether the object was allocated from a global or local storage pool, is used to avoid dangling references (described in Section 9.6).

Table 9-3 lists the instructions that operate on ADs. Note that ADs can be freely copied to the access part of any accessible segment. The INSPECT ACCESS DESCRIPTOR instruction copies the image of an AD to a segment's data part for examination. Of course, an AD image stored in a data part cannot be used as an AD.

Locating an Intel 432 object through an AD requires two steps. The AD, in addition to the rights bits, contains two indices: an index into the system-wide Object Table Directory

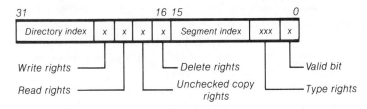

Figure 9-4: Intel 432 Access Descriptor

165

COPY ACCESS DESCRIPTOR

        Copies an AD from one segment's access part to another.

NULL ACCESS DESCRIPTOR

        Invalidates an AD.

INSPECT ACCESS DESCRIPTOR

        Copies the information in an AD into a segment's data part.

INSPECT OBJECT   Copies the information from an AD and the object descriptor to which it refers into a segment's data part.

AMPLIFY RIGHTS   Amplifies the rights in an AD under control of a Type Control Object.

RESTRICT RIGHTS   Removes rights specified by an AD.

CREATE OBJECT   Creates a segment with specified data part and access part lengths, and returns an AD for the segment.

CREATE TYPED OBJECT

        Creates a segment of the specified type with specified data part and access part lengths, and returns an AD for the segment.

Table 9-3:   Intel 432 Access Descriptor Instructions

and an index into an object table. This mapping is shown in Figure 9-5. The first index locates the object descriptor for an object table. The second index locates the object descriptor for the specified object in the selected table.

Each access to a byte in a segment potentially requires four references, one each to:

- the access descriptor in an access segment,
- the Object Table Directory,
- the object table, and
- the byte itself.

With the exception of the access to the AD, the two-level mapping overhead is comparable to the overhead required on any conventional virtual memory system. Of course, caches can be used to decrease this overhead substantially. The first implementation of the 432 has several small on-chip caches to remember recently used translations.

Since AD index fields are 12 bits, an object table can have a maximum of 4096 (2^{12}) object descriptors. In addition, there

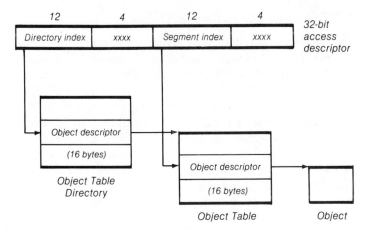

Figure 9-5: Intel 432 Address Translation

can be a maximum of 4096 object tables in the system at any time. Combined with the fact that a segment has a maximum size of 64K bytes, the total size of the address space is 2^{40} bytes. However, the maximum address space available to a procedure at any one time is 2^{32} bytes.

9.4 Program Execution

Several system objects exist to support the representation and execution of procedures on the Intel 432, including:

- the *domain object*, which defines a module, package, or set of related procedures,
- the *instruction object*, which defines a single executable procedure, and
- the *context object*, which provides the execution environment for an executing procedure.

These objects can be grouped into two classes—those that describe the *static* representation of procedures (the domain and instruction objects) and those that describe the *dynamic* execution of procedures (the context object). An instruction object corresponds to a Hydra procedure object, while the context object corresponds to a Hydra local name space object. At any time, there may be several context objects that represent different invocations of a single instruction object. The following sections describe these program objects in more detail.

167

9.4.1 Domains and Instruction Objects

A domain object, illustrated in Figure 9-6, contains ADs for the instruction objects and local objects used within a module. The Intel 432 architecture specifies the format of the first two ADs in a domain. These ADs address instruction objects that handle fault and trace conditions for all procedures in the domain. In the event of a fault or trace condition, the hardware automatically branches to the first instruction in the fault or trace object specified in the domain of the currently executing procedure. The remainder of a domain's access part contains ADs for procedures and objects needed by the domain; these ADs are defined by the software system (usually a compiler) creating the domain.

One of the objects typically addressed by a domain is a segment containing scalar constants used by the domain's procedures. Each instruction object, shown in Figure 9-6, contains the domain index of its scalar constants segment. This segment is needed because Intel 432 instructions do not have literal operand values embedded within the instruction stream. The instruction object also specifies the size of the context object to be produced as the result of the procedure call. The initial

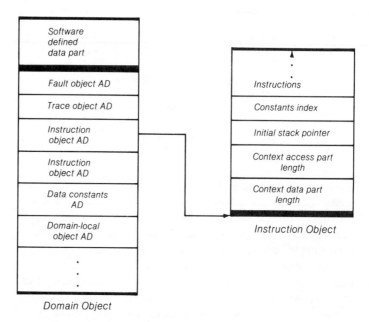

Domain Object

Instruction Object

Figure 9-6: Intel 432 Domain and Instruction Objects

stack pointer index is the displacement to the start of the data stack in the context object. The use of these fields will become apparent in the following discussion of context objects.

Instruction objects contain only a data part. Because Intel 432 instructions are bit-addressable and can start on arbitrary bit boundaries, instructions are addressed as bit offsets into instruction objects. The first instruction in each instruction object begins at bit displacement 64, following the header of four 16-bit predefined fields. The maximum size of an instruction segment is 64K bits, or 8K bytes, due to the bit addressing. Although there is generally one instruction object for each procedure in the domain, procedures larger than 8K bytes require additional instruction objects. The BRANCH INTERSEGMENT instruction can be used to transfer control to another instruction object within the same domain.

9.4.2 Procedure Call and Context Objects

To transfer control to a procedure, a program executes a CALL instruction, causing the procedure to be invoked. On execution of a CALL instruction, the hardware constructs a new context object. The context object is the procedure invocation record and defines the dynamic addressing environment in which the procedure executes. All addressing of objects and scalars occurs through the context object, and the context is the root of all objects reachable by the procedure. The structure of the context object is illustrated in Figure 9-7.

Although somewhat complicated, it is important to examine the context object in more detail to understand the addressing environment of the Intel 432. The context object has both a data part and an access part. The data part contains pointers that describe the current instruction execution. The domain index locates the AD for the executing instruction object within the current domain; the instruction pointer contains the bit offset of the current instruction in that instruction object. At the high-address end of the context object's data part is the operand stack. This stack is used by instructions for computation and intermediate storage of scalar values. The current stack pointer is also stored in the data part.

The context object's access part contains ADs that define the addressing environment for the procedure. Included are ADs for the *current domain*, which was specified by the CALL instruction, and the AD for the *local constants segment*, which was specified in the called instruction object. The *global con-*

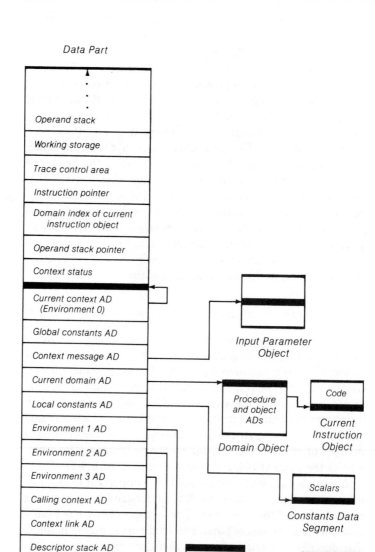

Figure 9-7: Intel 432 Context Object Representation

stants AD allows addressing of a process-wide data segment; the procedure explicitly loads this AD, if needed, through the COPY PROCESS GLOBALS instruction. The *calling context* AD addresses the caller so that a RETURN can be executed.

Interprocess communication is provided by instructions that send messages to and receive messages from port objects. Execution of a RECEIVE MESSAGE instruction causes the AD for the received message to be copied to the *interprocess message* AD in the context object's access part. In this way, the program has immediate addressability to the message. The *static link* AD, which follows the interprocess message AD in the context, is provided to support languages that use static lexical scoping.

9.4.3 Instruction Operand Addressing

The important context object ADs from the addressing point of view are those named *current context* and *environments 1, 2,* and *3* in Figure 9-7. As previously stated, an instruction must specify the location of an AD in order to manipulate any object. If the instruction manipulates one or more data elements, it must provide ADs for the segments containing those elements. In general, then, every instruction operand specifies one or more ADs that provide addressability to that operand.

At any moment during a procedure's execution, ADs specified by instructions must be located in one of four *environment objects*. Environment object 0 is the context object itself. Instructions can specify any of the ADs within the context object's access part; for example, to refer to the domain or the constants data segment. The three remaining environments, environments 1 through 3, are defined dynamically by the procedure. A procedure loads an AD for any object into the environment slots in the context object to make ADs in that object addressable. The ENTER ENVIRONMENT instructions are provided for this purpose.

Therefore, to address an AD, an instruction specifies one of the four environment objects and an index to an AD in the object's access part. Environment 0 is the context access part itself, which is self-addressed through the current context AD in the context object. Environments 1 through 3 are addressed through the three environment ADs in the context object. An instruction reference to an AD in one of the four environments is called an *access selector*. Figure 9-8 shows the three access selector formats. The low-order two bits in each selector spec-

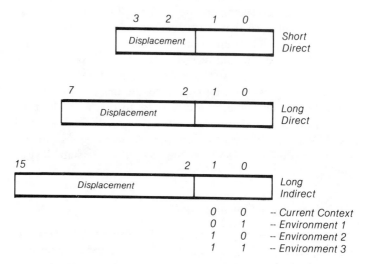

Figure 9-8: Intel 432 Access Selector Formats

ify the environment object; the three formats allow for 2-, 6-, or 14-bit displacements to an AD in the selected environment.

The four environment segments thus provide efficient addressing of ADs. An instruction can specify an immediate 4- or 8-bit access selector describing the location of an AD for an operand. Or, it can specify the location of a 16-bit access selector located in memory or on the stack. The short direct format efficiently addresses any of the first four ADs in any of the four environments. This includes the ADs for the global constants, context message (calling parameters), and current domain within the current context. All of the processor-defined ADs within the context object's access part can be addressed using an 8-bit access selector.

9.4.4 Context Allocation

On an earlier version of the Intel 432 architecture, each CALL instruction caused dynamic allocation of the memory segment in which the new context object was constructed. Because this allocation was time-consuming, the latest version of the Intel 432 supports preallocation of contexts on a per-process basis. The operating system allocates a linked list of fixed-sized context object segments to each process. The contexts are linked through the *context link* field in each context object. When a call occurs, the processor reads the context link field to find the AD for the next context object to use. The length of this object is compared with the length fields stored in the called instruction object. If the instruction object requires a context object larger than the preallocated size, a fault will occur. The operating system can then allocate a context of the needed size. Or, if the context link is null, indicating that the preallocated contexts have been consumed, a fault will allow the operating system to perform additional allocations. Otherwise, the hardware quickly constructs the new context object from the linked segment.

9.4.5 Parameter Passing

Parameter passing on the Intel 432 is associated with the preallocation of contexts and is handled by software. In addition to the default context object size, associated with each process is a default data part size and access part size of a *parameter segment* to be passed between contexts on procedure calls. However, instead of allocating a separate parameter segment, an area of the data part and access part of each context object is reserved for parameter passing. When the operating system constructs the linked list of contexts, it places in the *context message* field of each context, an AD for a *refinement* of the *previous* context object. This refinement provides addressability to the parameter data and access fields as if they were a single contiguous segment.

Figure 9-9 illustrates how a procedure accesses parameters passed by its caller. The calling procedure places its data and access parameters in the predefined parameter fields of its context object. The operating system had previously created a refinement object descriptor for these parameter spaces and placed an AD for the refinement in the next context object. When the call occurs, the called context can access its parameters through its context message AD.

9.5 Abstraction Support

The principal goal of the Intel 432 is support for object-based programming. As previously described, the Intel 432 provides a set of basic system object types. Each of the system object types is controlled by a type manager that is implemented partially in hardware—through a set of type-specific instructions—and partially in operating system software.

173

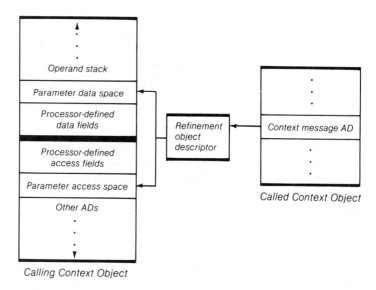

Figure 9-9: Intel 432 Parameter Passing

To extend the set of basic types, the Intel 432 provides mechanisms for the creation of programmer-defined types and programmer-defined type managers. Since all objects are accessed through a high-level language, the programmer uses the same interface when dealing with system objects and with programmer-defined objects. A programmer is free to create new types and type managers, adding to the set of available abstractions.

There are three system object types involved in type manager support:

- the domain, which defines the procedures and objects local to a single module of the type manager,
- the Type Control Object (TCO), which is used in creation of system and programmer-defined objects, and
- the Type Definition Object (TDO), which defines a particular type manager.

This section describes the use of these objects for the creation and manipulation of system and programmer-defined objects.

9.5.1 Domains and Refinements

A *domain* object defines a collection of procedures and associated objects accessible to those procedures. By using the 432 refinement mechanism, a programmer can create a protected procedure environment with a domain object. That is, a programmer can construct a set of callable procedures that will have access to objects not available to their callers.

Figure 9-10 shows a domain that consists of a collection of procedure ADs and object ADs. To construct a protected subsystem, the creator of the domain divides the domain into two sections: a public section and a private section. The public section consists of ADs for procedures that will be callable by users of the domain. The private section consists of ADs for procedures and objects that will be available only to called procedures executing within the domain.

Through the CREATE REFINEMENT instruction, the domain's owner constructs a refinement of the domain that addresses only the public section—the section that will be visible to users of the domain. The CREATE REFINEMENT instruction returns an AD for this refinement. The AD for the domain refinement can be made available to other programmers, who can use this AD to call any of the public procedures. However, a possessor of this refinement AD has access only to the domain's public part.

This use of domain refinement creates a protected subsystem because of the action of the CALL instruction. When a CALL instruction is executed, the hardware places an AD for the called domain in the new context object, where it is accessible to the called procedure. The hardware *always* loads an AD for

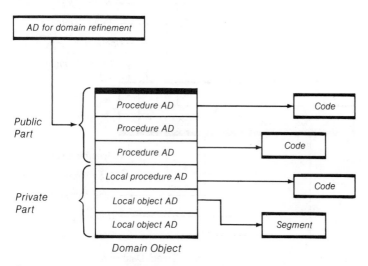

Figure 9-10: Intel 432 Domain Refinement

175

the *complete* domain, even if the CALL was made through a refinement. Therefore, a procedure invoked through a refinement of a domain will have access to all of the ADs in its domain through its context object. Once executing, the procedure can manipulate private data objects or call private domain procedures.

9.5.2 Creation of Typed Objects

The Intel 432 supports two kinds of object types: system types and programmer-defined types. The system types were listed previously in Table 9-1; instances of system types are identified by the 8-bit system type field in their object table object descriptors. Two of the system types are *generic object*, which is a basic segment object with no special attributes, and *dynamic object,* which is an object controlled by a programmer-defined type manager.

Typed objects of any kind are created through the CREATE TYPED OBJECT instruction. Execution of the CREATE TYPED OBJECT instruction requires possession of the AD for a *type control object* (TCO). A TCO permits its possessor to create and manipulate objects of a specific type. The data part of a TCO is illustrated in Figure 9-11.

Creation of a system object (with the exception of generic objects) requires possession of a TCO whose object type field

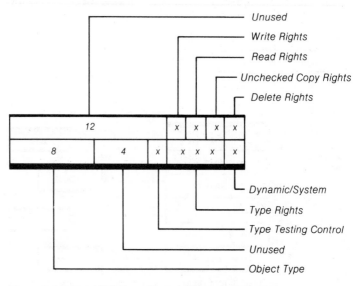

Figure 9-11: Intel 432 Type Control Object Data Part

contains the 8-bit type value of the system type to be created. In addition, the dynamic/system bit (bit 0) of the TCO must indicate that the TCO is for a system object. TCOs for the creation of specific system object types are constructed by the operating system and given to the operating system type managers for those types. The type manager for a system object is privileged only in its possession of the TCO for its type.

Possession of a TCO for a specific type also allows the type manager to execute an AMPLIFY RIGHTS instruction for objects of its type. In this way, the type manager can return restricted ADs to its clients. These restricted ADs cannot be used to access the objects to which they refer. When a client returns an AD to a type manager as a parameter, however, the type manager can use its TCO to amplify the rights in the AD. Given an AD for an object and an AD for a TCO with matching type, the AMPLIFY RIGHTS instruction ORs the rights bits specified in the TCO with the rights in the object AD, creating an AD with additional privileges. If the TCO and AD types do not match, the AMPLIFY RIGHTS instruction will cause a fault.

9.5.3 Programmer-Defined Types

To build a private type management system, a programmer obtains a *type definition object* (TDO) from the operating system. A TDO has no processor-defined fields, although its access part will typically be used to hold ADs for the domains that implement the type manager. The basic function of the TDO is to be the representative "type" for its objects. That is, while the type of a system object is specified by an 8-bit system object type field, the type of a dynamic object is specified by an AD for a TDO. All objects created by a specific type manager have an image of the AD for the type manager's TDO stored in their object table object descriptor (shown as TDO-AD in Figure 9-3).

Once a type manager has obtained a TDO, it then obtains a TCO from the operating system for its type. This TCO will be for a dynamic object, as specified in its system type field and in the dynamic/system field. A TCO for a dynamic object contains an additional field—a single AD in its access part. This is the AD for the defining TDO. When the type manager executes a CREATE TYPED OBJECT instruction to allocate a segment for the object's representation, it specifies its TCO and the size of the segment to allocate. The hardware copies the TDO access descriptor from the TCO into the object descriptor for the

177

new segment, thereby "typing" the segment. Figure 9-12 shows this addressing structure; the object descriptor for the new dynamic object contains the physical storage information for the object and the AD for the TDO.

The programmer-defined type manager, like the system object type manager, protects its objects using restriction and amplification. When a client requests the creation of a new object, the type manager creates the object using the CREATE TYPED OBJECT instruction. The type manager then initializes the object appropriately and uses the RESTRICT RIGHTS instruction to produce an AD to be returned to the client. This AD does not allow direct access to the object. When the client later specifies this AD as a parameter, the type manager amplifies rights in the AD to regain access to the object's representation. Once again, the key to amplification is the possession of a TCO. The type manager executes an AMPLIFY RIGHTS instruction specifying its private TCO and the AD for the object. If the TCO and the object descriptor for the object both contain the same TDO AD, the instruction will amplify the rights in the object AD.

It is not necessary for programs to maintain ADs for all possible type managers. Given an AD for an object, a program can execute the RETRIEVE TYPE DEFINITION instruction; this instruction returns the AD for the TDO associated with the object. With the TDO AD, the program can access the AD for the domain implementing the type manager and can call type management procedures available through that domain. The domain AD stored in the TDO will typically be a refinement of the type manager's domain.

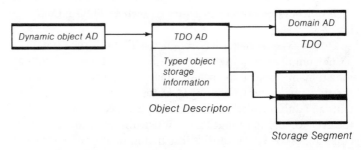

Figure 9-12: Intel 432 Dynamic Object Addressing

Previous sections have described the creation of storage segments through the CREATE OBJECT and CREATE TYPED OBJECT instructions; however, they have not described the mechanism by which primary memory is allocated. The abstraction of primary storage is encapsulated in Intel 432 *storage resource objects*. A storage resource object (SRO) is a system object from which memory is allocated. Every memory allocation instruction specifies, either explicitly or by default, an SRO from which its primary memory is taken.

Figure 9-13 illustrates the structure of an SRO and its associated objects. The representation of an SRO consists principally of the AD for a *physical storage object* that describes a pool of available primary memory, and an AD for an object table. Each storage specifier in the physical storage object contains the primary memory address and size of a single contiguous block of free system memory. Initially, each physical storage object has one storage specifier for a single large block. As storage is dynamically allocated and deallocated from an SRO, its memory becomes fragmented and new storage specifiers must be created to address the discontiguous pieces.

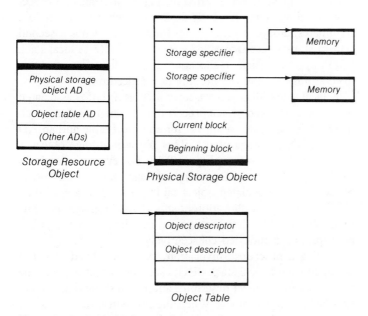

Figure 9-13: Intel 432 Storage Resource Object

When a program executes a CREATE OBJECT instruction, it specifies an SRO from which the storage is to be taken. The hardware allocates primary memory on a rotating first-fit basis from the SRO's storage specifiers. After allocating the memory, the hardware allocates an object descriptor for the new object in the SRO's object table; an AD is returned that addresses the object through that object descriptor.

The SRO in Figure 9-13 is known as a *global heap SRO* and is used to allocate relatively long-lived objects. Storage allocated from a global SRO can be returned at any time. The SRO's object table contains a descriptor that is the head of a list of unused object descriptors in the table. This list is used both for locating an empty table slot when an object is created and for returning an object descriptor when an object is destroyed. Returned storage is either combined with an adjacent free block in the SRO, or a new storage specifier is constructed to address it.

Global heap SROs provide great flexibility for dynamic storage allocation. The disadvantage of global heaps, however, is that they require garbage collection for deallocation of storage. Although the overhead of garbage collection is acceptable for long-lived objects, it is prohibitive for short-lived objects. In particular, most objects created during the lifetime of a procedure could be more efficiently deallocated when the procedure terminates. For this reason, the Intel 432 provides a second type of storage resource called a *local stack SRO*. A local stack SRO supports efficient allocation and deallocation of short-lived storage during the lifetime of a procedure.

A local stack SRO is not a separate object, but is associated with a process object. Each process object contains a local stack SRO, which consists of an AD for an object table and an AD for a physical storage object. This physical storage object is similar to that shown in Figure 9-13; however, it contains a *single* storage specifier for a *single* storage block. This storage block and the associated object table are used in a stack-like (LIFO) fashion for allocation of short-lived local storage. The local object table does not use a free list; instead, object descriptors are allocated consecutively.

During a procedure invocation, each short-lived object is allocated from a local stack SRO; each new object receives the next contiguous object descriptor and the next contiguous section of the storage block. When the procedure returns, all of the objects and object descriptors for short-term objects created by the procedure can be deallocated. This deallocation is simple when compared with global heap deallocation because both the object table and storage block are managed as stacks. All of the short-term objects and descriptors allocated during a procedure call can be quickly deallocated by returning the object table and physical storage objects to their pre-call states.

Local stack SROs are therefore more efficient for allocation and deallocation than global heap SROs, although they cannot accommodate objects of different lifetimes. The more difficult problem presented by local stack SROs is the control of ADs for local objects. Objects allocated from global heap SROs are only deallocated by a garbage collector. The garbage collector ensures that no ADs remain for an object before its storage and object descriptor are deallocated. If an object with an existing AD were deallocated, the AD would become a dangling reference. For example, suppose that AD X addresses object Y through object descriptor Z. If object Y and object descriptor Z are deallocated while X still exists, AD X will be a dangling reference. Eventually, object descriptor Z will be reused to address a newly created object, and AD X could be used erroneously to access that object.

This problem is compounded in the case of local stack SROs by the rate at which object descriptors are reused. An object descriptor deallocated by a procedure return will very likely be reused by the next procedure call. Therefore, the Intel 432 must be able to ensure that when a procedure returns, no ADs remain for short-term objects allocated during that call. To prevent such dangling references, the Intel 432 controls the propagation of ADs. The hardware prevents the storing of an AD into a segment whose lifetime is longer than the lifetime of the object addressed by that AD.

The lifetime of an object is determined by the *level number* stored in its object descriptor. Each process has a current level number; the level number is first initialized when the process is created and is incremented by one at each procedure call. When an object is created, the current level number is stored in its object descriptor. An attempt to copy an AD for an object created at level N into a segment created at level N-1 or lower will cause a fault. When an object allocated from a local stack SRO is destroyed on procedure return, the system can guarantee that no ADs for that object remain; that is, all of the storage into which the AD could have been copied must have been destroyed when the object was destroyed.

Any object that is to be passed to other processes or stored in a more global segment must be allocated from a global heap

SRO instead of the default local stack SRO. The architecture ensures that only correct copying of ADs takes place. The unchecked copy rights bit in Intel 432 ADs provides an optimization for the required level check. The unchecked copy flag indicates whether the object was allocated from a level-0 global heap. If so the level check can be avoided; otherwise, the level numbers in the object descriptors must be checked.

9.7 Instructions

The Intel 432 has a repertoire of about 225 instructions that operate on characters, integers, floating point numbers, and system objects. There are no general registers. Each context has a private operand stack that can be used for storing scalar temporaries. Scalar operands for instructions can be located either on the stack or in memory, and memory-to-memory operations are allowed.

One of the unique features of the Intel 432 is its instruction encoding. Instructions are bit-variable in length and can start on any bit boundary. The instruction pointer thus contains the bit offset into the current instruction segment, which can be up to 8K bytes in size. An instruction consists of up to four fields, as shown in Figure 9-14. The fields themselves are also variable-length and highly encoded.

The 4- to 6-bit *class* field specifies the number of operands and their sizes. For example, the class may indicate that an instruction requires three 32-bit operands or two 16-bit operands. Next, the 0- to 4-bit *format* field specifies whether each of the operands is (1) to be found on the stack or (2) to be specified explicitly by a reference in the references field, and (3) if specified explicitly, which reference corresponds to which operand. The *references* field specifies where the (one to three) operands are to be found. A stack operand requires no reference field entry, and a single reference may refer to two operands, as specified by the format field. For example, an operand that is both a source and destination requires only one reference field to define its location. Finally, the 0- to 5-bit *opcode* specifies the operation to perform.

Opcode	References	Format	Class

Least Significant Bit

Figure 9-14: Intel 432 Instruction Format

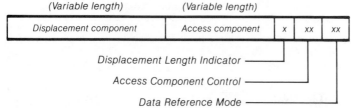

Figure 9-15: Intel 432 Reference Format

The references field is the most important with respect to object addressing and requires the most complex encoding. The size of the references field depends on the number of operand references and the addressing mode for each. An instruction operand can be either a *scalar operand* (e.g., integer, character, floating point) or an *object-level operand* (e.g., process, domain, message port). If the instruction operand requires a scalar, the reference specifies its location. If the instruction operand requires an object-level operator, the reference specifies an AD for the object.

The general format of a single reference is shown in Figure 9-15. The length and format of the variable-length access and displacement components are determined by the leading control fields. For example, in the case of a scalar operand, the instruction must specify two components needed to locate the scalar:

- the location of an AD for the object containing the scalar, and
- the displacement of the scalar within the object's data part.

The access component field locates the AD for the object; it is a 4- or 8-bit field whose format was shown in Figure 9-8. The displacement component, in the simplest addressing mode, is a 7- or 16-bit integer displacement.

Several addressing modes are allowed that provide for indirect specification of the access and displacement components; that is, the access and displacement specifications for the reference can be found in memory. For example, in the case of an indirectly specified displacement, the displacement field of the reference must itself contain an access and displacement part. Such general addressing modes provide for flexibility but can require many memory accesses in order to manipulate a single data element. Thus, a reference to an element of a dynamically allocated one-dimensional array might indicate:

183

- an access selector for the segment containing the array,
- the displacement of the array in the segment,
- an access selector for a possibly different segment containing the array index, and
- a displacement of the index in this second segment.

Many options are provided for each part of the specification and, in general, commonly occurring options can be efficiently encoded. Stack operands save the most instruction space because they require no reference field bits. Space can also be saved in the reference field if operands are located at the start of a segment because this requires no offset. There is a large variance in instruction size—a three-operand instruction can take from 10 to more than 300 bits, depending on where the operands are to be found.

9.8 Discussion

The Intel iAPX 432 is certainly one of the most sophisticated architectures in existence. By using the object-oriented approach throughout the development effort, the Intel 432 designers have produced an extremely uniform and tightly-integrated hardware/software system. This uniformity of hardware and software systems is due to the use of a consistent philosophy. Everything in the Intel 432 is an object. All objects have associated types that specify the operations that can be performed on those objects. Some objects have hardware-defined operations while others do not. However, from a language viewpoint, all objects are accessed in the same way.

All objects, whether hardware-supported or not, are controlled by type manager modules. Programmers can freely add new types to the system by creating new type managers. The mechanisms of domain refinement and type definition object provide a way for type managers to exhibit privilege over their objects and the environments in which their procedures execute. A type manager can restrict and later amplify privileges in ADs for its objects by using a privately held type control object. By permitting client access to type management procedures through a refinement, an executing type management procedure can obtain access to a richer environment than its caller.

There are no special privileges in the Intel 432 system. The mechanisms used by programmer-defined type managers are identical to those used by operating system type managers.

In addition, the concept of programmer-defined type is an integral part of the addressing system, in that each object descriptor has space for a TDO access descriptor. Few previous systems have allocated sufficient space to integrate programmer-defined objects so tightly into the hardware architecture.

The designers of the Intel 432 have closely adhered to the concept of separate procedure address spaces, as presented in the Dennis and Van Horn model. Each procedure invocation causes the construction of a new context object that defines the procedure's addressing environment. This is true even of calls to procedures within the same domain, for which both procedures will have access to a similar set of objects.

Although an initial implementation of the Intel 432 had separate data segments and capability segments, the current version supports segments with both a data part and a capability part, as on STAROS. The object descriptor addresses the barrier between the two parts and contains the size of each part. Refinements are provided that allow the construction of what appears to be a single two-part segment from contiguous subsets of the two parts of a segment. Two-part segments do not allow the flexibility provided by tagging; however, they effectively reduce the number of needed segments by a factor of two. This affects performance by reducing the number of segment allocations required to create a new object.

Another performance enhancement has resulted from the preallocation of context objects. When a procedure call occurs, the hardware simply follows the context link to the next waiting context object. That object has already been prepared with a refinement of the parameter space in the calling context. In addition, the use of local stack SROs for allocating short-lived objects reduces the need for garbage collection. These changes to the CALL instruction have reduced its execution time from 300 microseconds on early prototypes to under 100 microseconds on the current version of the Intel 432.

Capabilities on the Intel 432 are 32 bits in size. Of this, 24 bits form the actual ID or address part of the capability. Thus, there are a maximum of 2^{24} objects at any time. Segments have a maximum (data part) size of 64K, which is relatively small when compounded by the lack of cross-segment addressing. That is, due to the structure of Intel 432 addresses, it is not possible to transparently cross a segment boundary by incrementing the address. Therefore, the compiler must produce special code for objects whose data parts cannot be held in a single segment. This is true also of procedures that are larger than 8K bytes, although this is probably a rare occurrence.

The instantaneous address space of the Intel 432 is 2^{32} bytes, based on the use of the four environment ADs stored in the context object. These environment ADs act somewhat like capability registers, and, in fact, the Intel 432 GDP has special internal registers to hold their values. At any time, ADs in use by a procedure must be stored in one of the four environment objects. To access objects located indirectly through the environments, the procedure must explicitly traverse the structure, loading ADs for each level in the tree.

The Intel iAPX 432 is an ambitious system in terms of both architecture and implementation. It is particularly impressive when considered in relation to the other available single-chip processors. But it is fair to say that the Intel 432 has not been a commercial success. Although there were over 100 Intel 432 systems in the hands of universities and customers by 1983, this is a small number by microprocessor standards. The commercial problems of the Intel 432 are probably due in part to premature (and somewhat overzealous) marketing of the product before its implementation and software were ready. The initial version of the Intel 432 had performance problems, which have been corrected to some extent by later versions of the architecture. Still, whether or not the Intel 432 succeeds as a product, it has opened a new era of microprocessor design.

9.9 For Further Reading

The book by [Organick 83] presents the most comprehensive description of the Intel 432. It describes the major components of the Intel 432 system—the Ada compiler, the iMAX operating system, and the iAPX 432 hardware architecture—and provides Ada programming examples as well. In the published literature, the paper by Pollack, Kahn, and Wilkinson describes the philosophy behind the Intel 432 object filing system [Pollack 81], and the paper by Cox, Korwin, Lai, and Pollack discusses the Intel 432 interprocess communication facility used for both message passing and process scheduling [Cox 83]. Storage management on the Intel 432 is discussed in [Pollack 82]. The Architecture Reference Manual [Intel 81, Intel 82] contains detailed descriptions of the Intel 432 architecture.

Issues in Capability-Based Architectures

10.1 Introduction

Previous chapters have followed the transition from early descriptor-based computer architectures to the latest in commercially available capability systems. The examination began with the Burroughs B5000 and the Rice University computer. Both of these machines used descriptors, or user-addressable base/limit registers, to define a program's addressing environment. Capability systems extended this idea in several significant ways:

1. Capabilities are *protected addresses*. They can be freely copied, passed as parameters, and transmitted from domain to domain, but cannot be forged or modified by users.
2. Capabilities are *context-independent*. They address the same object independent of the domain or process in which they are used.
3. Capabilities contain access rights as well as addressing information.
4. The address or identifier in a capability is independent of the physical base and limit information used for memory mapping. This identifier is used to locate a single physical descriptor for the addressed object.
5. Capabilities and the objects they address can be saved in long-term storage. They have a lifetime longer than the existence of the process that created them.
6. Capabilities provide a uniform mechanism for *naming* all types of objects in the environment, both hardware and software supported. This enables users to extend the facilities provided by the hardware and vendor-supplied operating system software. Moreover, they provide run-time support for abstraction and object-based programming.

Of course, these capability concepts did not appear at once but evolved over time. Each new system was able to benefit from experience gained in previous systems—even those that were short-lived.

This chapter discusses some of the design issues in capability-based systems. Although each topic could be a chapter in itself, the discussions here are relatively brief. Where possible, tradeoffs are examined in the light of the various systems described.

10.2 Segmentation

This book began by examining the objectives of early systems in diverging from the conventional linear address space. Because each of the systems examined includes a segmented memory space, it is fitting to begin the discussion with a review of segmentation. Segments are the fundamental objects in capability systems; they provide the units of addressing and sharing.

The reasons for segmentation are much the same today as they were in 1960:

1. Segments correspond to logical program entities. They can be used to decompose programs and data structures into units that are meaningful to the programmer.
2. Segmentation allows the logical entities to grow or shrink.
3. Segmentation supports memory relocation and virtual storage.
4. Segments provide logical units of separation, protection, and sharing, both between programs and processes and within a single program or process. Moreover, segments allow for a dynamically changing memory environment.

On early machines, a segment was addressed through a descriptor—usually contained in a descriptor segment. Iliffe's Basic Language Machine included a type for each segment to indicate the kind of information contained there. The type was stored in the descriptor for a segment; it allowed automatic conversion and tagging when data elements were moved from memory into registers.

On current object-based machines, abstract objects are composed of one or more segments. For multisegment objects, a capability for a base segment serves to address the object as a whole. This base segment contains pointers to the other segments forming the object. Segments are thus the basic units addressed by capabilities.

Although segments are the fundamental units of storage allocation, paging can be provided along with segmentation, as in the IBM System/38. Each segment is divided into fixed-sized pages that can be independently located. Paging adds additional storage overhead for the system data structures that maintain information about the memory state. However, the division of physical and virtual storage into fixed-sized units simplifies memory management by removing the memory shuffling and compacting problems.

10.3 Storage of Capabilities

Capability systems have no privileged mode of operation. All privileges, including those permitted to the operating system, are derived from the possession of capabilities. The integrity of the entire system depends on the fact that users cannot forge capabilities or modify them directly. For this reason, the hardware must be able to detect and prohibit any attempt to modify a capability with data instructions. Two different schemes have been used to provide this capability protection: C-lists and tagging.

Most systems have chosen to implement C-lists—often implemented as capability segments—to protect capabilities. Using this protection mechanism, capabilities are stored only in capability segments where they are segregated from user-modifiable data. Separation of capabilities can complicate the construction of record-oriented data structures in which it is natural to mix data and pointers (capabilities). However, a compiler can mask this problem by implementing the structure in two parts or by storing a specifier for the capability, such as the C-list index, instead of the capability itself.

The implementation of C-lists is technologically simpler than tagging; it requires no special hardware on a per-information-unit basis. A single bit in the physical mapping information for each segment indicates whether the segment contains capabilities or data. Or, as is often the case, the distinction is maintained in the access rights of capabilities used to address a segment. Each segment capability indicates whether capability or data access is allowed to that segment. The operating system is privileged because it possesses capabilities that allow data access to user's capability segments.

In addition to implementation advantages, C-lists can provide added efficiency in capability addressing. For example, capabilities can be specified by their index in a C-list. If multi-

189

ple C-lists are allowed, then multiple indices may be needed. Or, if the number of directly addressable capability segments can be restricted (e.g., the Intel 432's 4 environments or CAP's 16 capability segments), a small number of bits appended to the index can specify which C-list to use. Short forms of addressing can be provided for cases where the most frequently used capabilities are stored at small displacements from the start of the C-list. Thus, C-list schemes often result in a reduction of the number of bits needed to refer to a capability, as compared to the number of bits needed for a general memory address.

The second method of capability protection requires the use of tag bits. Tagging allows capabilities to be stored with user data. The ability to combine capabilities and data can simplify data structuring for the user. Tagging probably has not been used much in the past because of the added memory cost and implementation complexity. Still, several early descriptor systems used tagging when memory was scarce. Certainly memory cost should not be an issue today.

The storage cost of tagging depends on the size of the tagged information units: the smaller the tagged unit the greater the overhead. Most modern systems are byte addressable, but tagging on a byte basis is probably overly expensive. On the System/38 there is one tag bit for each 32-bit word. In a case where tags are not provided on the smallest addressable information unit, capabilities must be aligned on the boundary of a tagged unit, such as a 32-bit word. If capabilities are larger than the tagged unit, as they are with 16-byte System/38 capabilities, alignment must be on larger units.

The System/38 requires that capabilities be aligned on 16-byte boundaries and that the tag bits associated with the four consecutive words be set. The alignment requirement prohibits a user from addressing four consecutive tagged words that do not form a valid capability. For example, two consecutively stored capabilities will cause eight tag bits to be set. A user could address four consecutive words consisting of the last two words of the first capability and the first two words of the second capability. This four-word item is not a valid capability even though the associated tags are set. The alignment requirement could be eliminated at the cost of a second tag bit with each 32-bit word. The second tag bit would indicate whether or not the associated word is the first word of a multi-word capability.

Tag bits can be either part of a data element, which reduces the number of bits in the element, or part of a special storage area associated with each element. The System/38 chose to store the tags outside of the data element in an area accessible only to microcode. When a segment is written to disk, the hardware extracts the tags and stores them in a compact form along with the segment. They are later reinserted when the segment is read back into memory.

STAROS and the Intel 432 have chosen a scheme combining advantages of both tagging and C-lists. These systems support two-part segments that contain a data portion and a capability portion. The descriptor for the segment indicates the size of each portion and the position of the dividing line. Addressing occurs as with separate segments; the type of an operand determines in which portion it is contained. This design reduces the number of segments and mapping descriptors. Since most objects require both a data part and a capability part, the two-part segment scheme halves the number of segments needed to hold an object's representation.

The tagged memory approach is appealing in terms of generality; it allows capabilities to be freely mixed with data, just as pointers or addresses are freely mixed in virtual memory systems. A single stack can serve for local storage of both data and capabilities. The actual implementation of a tagging scheme has a number of complexities. The C-list approach is appealing in its simple implementation and in the addressing efficiencies that can be gained. C-lists can reduce the number of bits needed to address capabilities. Another advantage of C-lists (which will become apparent in later sections) is that they reduce the time required to search for capabilities.

In his comparison of the two techniques, Fabry claims that:

> ...the advantages of the partition approach are all technological, while some of its disadvantages are intrinsic. Thus one might expect the tagged approach to dominate in the long run [Fabry 74].

It may be too soon to tell, but so far, the partition (C-list) approach has dominated. Credit is probably due to current high-level languages, whose use masks the intrinsic disadvantages of C-lists.

10.4 Capability Representation

A fundamental decision in capability system design is the physical representation of capabilities. A capability contains two parts:

1. an identifier or name for an object, and

2. some access rights or privileges to that object.

The implementation of these fields influences the generality with which the capability can be applied, the work required to manage capabilities in both hardware and software, and the lifetime of objects and capabilities. In evaluating the evolution of the DEC PDP-11 minicomputer, Bell and Strecker state that:

> There is only one mistake that can be made in a computer design that is difficult to recover from—not providing enough address bits for memory addressing and memory management [Bell 76].

This applies to capability systems as well as conventional computers such as the PDP-11. The capability identifier corresponds directly to the address on conventional machines.

Early descriptor and codeword machines used single-word descriptors to address segments. Each descriptor contained all of the mapping information for the segment. Copying of a descriptor caused duplication of the mapping information. This duplication of memory base and limit values for a single segment added complexity to the task of relocation, which the descriptor was meant to simplify.

Two characteristics of these machines simplified the implementation of descriptors. First, the machines had large words and were word addressable. Second, they had relatively small memory spaces. Therefore, the base and limit information could be easily packed into a single word of the word-addressable machine. This removed the need for special alignment of descriptors.

New capability systems must contend with smaller word sizes, larger address spaces, byte addressability, and the greater volume of information needed to manage the system efficiently (e.g., usage and garbage collection bits). An additional problem is the long lifetime of objects on capability systems, in contrast to conventional machines where an object only exists for the lifetime of a program. The longer the object lifetime, the more bits needed for an object's address. These issues have forced an important distinction between the capability itself and the physical mapping information for the object. Thus, we see a separation between the capability, which contains an identifier, and the mapping descriptor, which is generally located in a centralized system table. This distinction is exemplified in the separation of information between Intel 432 access descriptors and object descriptors.

An important component of capability operation is the structure of the identifier. Each object or segment is given an ID at the time of its creation. This ID is often generated by a sequential counter, a clock, a disk address, or the values of indices used to locate the object's descriptor. The number of bits in the ID partly determines the number of objects that can exist at one time. Depending on the number of bits used, the ID can be unique for all time, unique for the life of the object, or unique during the object's residency in primary memory. Each of the possibilities has potential problems.

On most capability systems an object's ID is a direct index into a system mapping table. The mapping table contains descriptors for the object, giving its physical location, size, and so on. For example, capabilities on the Plessey 250 contain a 16-bit index into the System Capability Table. The use of this index as an object's ID places two restrictions on the system. First, the maximum number of addressable segments (at least in primary memory) at any one time is 2^{16} or 64K. Second, the System Capability Table must always be resident in physical memory. On the Plessey 250, the mapping table for 64K descriptors occupies about 589K bytes of storage.

The Intel 432 uses a two-level indexing structure, where the ID is 24 bits, allowing for 16 million objects. The 24-bit ID is divided into two 12-bit table indices. The first selects a descriptor in the central Object Table Directory. This descriptor addresses an object table in which the second index locates the descriptor for the object (this structure was shown in Figure 9-5). The two-level scheme allows the second-level object tables to be swapped out, reducing the amount of required storage overhead. Only the Object Table Directory, which has a maximum size of 64K bytes, need always be memory resident.

Both the Plessey and Intel mechanisms provide for a limited number of objects relative to the lifetime of the system. Therefore, object IDs must be reused when objects are destroyed. One problem with reuse of IDs is knowing what IDs are available to be reused. Since an object's ID is an index in the mapping table, a linked list of free table slots can be kept and used to assign new IDs and descriptors. When a new object is created, a free descriptor is taken and its index becomes the object's ID.

A second problem with reusable IDs is dangling references. When an object is deleted, outstanding capabilities for that object will still reference the mapping table descriptor slot for the object. If a new object is assigned to that descriptor slot, the old object's capability could be used to gain access to the new object. This implies that (1) an object cannot be deleted (or its descriptor reallocated) while capabilities exist for the object, or (2) all capabilities for an object to be deleted must be found and disabled. This problem is discussed further in Section 10.7 on object lifetimes and garbage collection.

Several capability systems have tried to alleviate the problems inherent in indexing schemes by implementing a unique-for-all-time ID space. On such systems, the ID is sufficiently large that the IDs are never used up. For example, object IDs on Hydra are 64 bits, allowing for over 10^{19} objects (it is left as an exercise for the reader to determine how long this address space would last if the system creates, for example, 100 new objects every millisecond). The IBM System/38 architecture also provides a large address space. A 40-bit ID, or segment number, provides for over one trillion segments. This number of segments is not likely to be consumed in the lifetime of most systems. Another unusual feature of the System/38 is that capabilities contain a virtual address that can reference a specific byte. In contrast, on most systems the capability identifies a segment, and a separate byte offset must be supplied independently. This feature is reminiscent of the earlier descriptor machines.

Of course, with a large address space, locating an object's descriptor from its unique ID is more complex than with direct indexing. The Hydra system hashes the unique ID to select one of 128 lists of active object entries in the Active Global Symbol Table. If the object is not found, a search of the Passive Global Symbol Table is made. Because the IBM System/38 uses paging, mapping information is associated with each page of a segment. A Page Directory Table contains the unique virtual page number of each page of primary memory. A hashed lookup is made in the Page Directory Table. If the lookup fails, a page fault occurs and the page must be read in from disk. System/38 capabilities retain the same form whether or not the segment is in primary memory.

All of these schemes require a one- or two-level table lookup to translate a capability identifier into a memory address. This overhead is comparable to the overhead involved in any segmented or virtual memory system. However, access via capabilities may incur additional overheads in order to validate type, access rights, and offset. Also, schemes that allow indirection in capabilities may require additional lookups. On the IBM System/38, some references require a user profile search to validate access rights to the object. References on the Intel 432 may require access to an object selector in memory that specifies the location of a capability operand. Those systems that do not have explicit or implicit capability registers always require an extra memory reference to fetch the capability from memory.

With the use of caches, translation buffers, and other processor-internal registers, there are probably no inherent performance disadvantages of capability system addressing relative to conventional virtual memory systems. All sophisticated modern systems require several levels of addressing indirection and rely on specialized high-speed memory to reduce the apparent overhead.

10.5 Objects

One of the more interesting developments in computer architecture is the relationship between capability hardware and object-based software. Capabilities provide a uniform naming mechanism for all types of objects. In addition to simple segments, capabilities are used to address abstract objects whose representations are stored in segments. This ability to uniformly address complex objects allows the programmer to extend the architectural interface in order to support high-level operating system or application functions.

All object-based systems supply a basic set of system objects. These objects usually provide for low-level resource management and interprocess communication. For example, message ports and processes are common system-supported objects. The IBM System/38 also includes a number of system objects that aid in the construction of database systems. Hardware support of object operations increases performance and hides object implementation.

One possible disadvantage of supporting many objects at the hardware level is the added complexity of the machine. The Intel 432 and IBM System/38 architectures are surely among the most complex in existence. The chances for error in hardware or microcode design and implementation are great. In addition, any high-level mechanism that is moved into hardware must be carefully considered. Because the mechanism and its interface cannot easily be changed, an ill-designed mechanism will simply waste valuable resources. The tradeoff

195

of whether or not to support a particular type in hardware is one of performance and integrity versus machine complexity.

10.6 Protected Procedures and Type Extension

One of the strengths of capability systems is that they allow operating systems and users to extend the hardware interface in a uniform way. This facility is available because capabilities can address operating system and user-implemented objects, as well as hardware supported objects. The only difference is that software-implemented operations are obtained through a CALL or ENTER instruction, while hardware-implemented operations are obtained through hardware instructions.

There are several requirements for a system that allows users to construct their own type managers: that is, protected subsystems that create and manipulate protected objects.

1. A user must be able to construct a type manager: an execution environment consisting of type management procedures and private data segments and objects. This private environment is usually called a domain. The domain is the static representation of the type management system.

2. The type manager must be able to distribute controlled access for its execution environment to its clients. Access is passed through a capability that permits invocation of public procedures but gives no access to any of the private objects in the domain.

3. The hardware must supply a mechanism to invoke the environment. Using the capability for the domain, a client must be able to cause execution of one of the public procedures in the domain. The invocation creates the dynamic type management environment in which the executing procedure has access to domain-local procedures and objects not available to its caller.

4. A type management procedure executing within the domain must be able to create new objects. It must be able to allocate segments in which the representation for new objects can be stored.

5. A type management procedure must be able to return to a client a *sealed capability* for an object. The sealing mechanism must prohibit the client from directly accessing the object's representation. Thus, the client holds the capability as proof of ownership and can pass it on to other users. Any operations on the object are performed by passing the capability as a calling parameter to a type management procedure. The type manager must retain the privilege to *unseal* capabilities of its type, thus gaining access to their representations.

Capability systems have implemented the addressing of programmer-defined type managers in several ways. One common mechanism is to provide a new instance of the type manager for each new object. When an object is created, the type manager returns an enter capability for a new instance of itself. This capability addresses a domain that includes capabilities for type management procedures along with a capability for the representation of the new object instance. The object is manipulated by calling type management procedures through the returned domain capability. The Plessey System 250 Central Capability Block and CAP Enter PRL scheme are examples of this mechanism.

A second mechanism is the use of restriction and amplification of capabilities. The type manager returns restricted capabilities for new object instances to its clients. These restricted capabilities cannot be used to access an object's representation, although they contain type-specific rights. The type manager retains a private capability that permits it to amplify all capabilities of its type. Clients of such a type manager must either have a separate capability for the type management domain or be able to access the domain indirectly through the object capability. The Hydra and Intel 432 systems use restriction and amplification. The Hydra TYPECALL mechanism allows the possessor of the capability for an object to call the object's type manager. The Intel 432 RETRIEVE TYPE DEFINITION instruction returns to the caller a capability for the type management domain of a specified object capability.

Whatever the mechanism, a system must be able to (1) define a procedure execution environment that is distinct from the environment in which the procedure was called and (2) protect the representation of an object so that only its type manager can directly modify its storage. A system that permits users to create such environments simplifies the construction and extension of operating systems by eliminating the notion of privilege that exists in conventional systems. Thus, modules traditionally constructed as part of a monolithic privileged kernel can be implemented and debugged independently as user programs.

10.7 Object Lifetimes and Garbage Collection

The object concept has dramatically changed the conventional concept of secondary storage. Traditional systems have stream-, record-, or block-oriented file systems that preserve information. Program-addressable entities are by default not long-lived; preservation of short-lived entities requires that they be converted to a format acceptable to the file system. On object-based systems, it is natural to wish to preserve objects on secondary storage—that is, to provide a virtual object storage system.

Many capability systems distinguish temporary and permanent objects. The CAL-TSS system became overly complex to some extent because of the decision not to handle secondary memory in the kernel and the inability to name temporary objects in the same way as permanent objects. Plessey 250 provided a virtual segment interface to the user and handled storage of capability segments on disk. Hydra presented a large, flat, object address space. Object storage is provided by both the System/38 and the Intel 432. Both of these systems also have temporary objects that have special treatment. The System/38 reserves part of its address space for temporary objects; these objects do not receive normal protection and are deleted when the system is booted. The Intel 432 gives temporary status to objects allocated out of local stack storage; these objects are implicitly deleted when the procedure in which they are allocated returns.

Object destruction is a difficult problem in capability systems. On the System/38, each object has an owner and the owner can delete the object explicitly. However, on most capability systems there is no concept of an object's owner. An object has some number of users, and each user possesses a capability for the object. Since capabilities can be easily deleted or passed from user to user, the set of users for an object can change dynamically.

It is often difficult to tell when an object is no longer needed. Garbage objects must be deleted or the system's disk or memory will eventually overflow with useless objects. The solution to this problem is garbage collection. A garbage collection process (or processes) is responsible for finding and deleting garbage objects. An object is garbage when it can no longer be accessed by any user. In the simplest case, if all capabilities for the object have been deleted, the object can never be referenced and can safely be destroyed.

One method of garbage detection is to maintain a reference count with each object. The reference count indicates the number of capabilities for the object and must be updated whenever a capability for the object is copied or deleted. When a reference count is decremented to zero, the object can be deleted.

There are at least two problems with reference counts that make them insufficient to solve the garbage collection problem completely. First, circularities can exist in the object structure. For example, if object A contains a capability for object B, while object B contains a capability for object A, then both will have reference counts of at least one. However, if no other capabilities exist for either object, then A and B are not accessible and should be deleted. Second, it is difficult to maintain the integrity of reference counts over system crashes. It would be costly to update a reference count on secondary storage for each capability copy or delete operation. If reference counts are only updated periodically on disk, a system crash can introduce inconsistencies.

Object-based systems must, therefore, resort to garbage collection. A simplified garbage collector would operate as follows. The garbage collection process starts with a set of root objects. In general, each user of the system has a principal C-list or directory that is the root of all objects the user can access; these lists or directories form the roots. The garbage collector first marks every object in the system as being unreachable (there must be some way of locating all objects through a master directory). The garbage collector then marks all objects in the root directories as being reachable. The C-lists of these objects must then be scanned to see if they refer to other objects to be marked as reachable, and so on recursively. Eventually all objects will be marked as reachable or unreachable, and a pass can be made to delete the unreachable objects.

Garbage collection is complex because it must operate concurrently with normal system processing. That is, a garbage collector must operate while objects and capabilities are being created, copied, and deleted. On some systems, such as STAROS, the garbage collector must be concerned with partitioning of the system. It must be able to operate while some nodes are unreachable and still guarantee that it will not delete an accessible object (worse than not deleting a garbage object). Similar problems exist on any system with multiple secondary storage devices in which one or more devices can be off-line at a given time. The garbage collector must be capable of finding objects that are not referenced at all, as well as objects that are members of unreachable cycles. Studies of garbage collection systems and algorithms can be found in [Bishop 77], [Dijkstra 78], and [Almes 80].

A related problem is garbage collection of the address space; that is, the reuse of descriptor slots in object mapping tables, such as the Plessey 250 System Capability Table and the Intel

432 object tables. These table slots must be reallocated because the table, which must be resident in physical memory, cannot map all objects known to the system. Therefore, on most systems, the mapping tables are used only to hold descriptors for objects resident in primary memory. This implies that an object can have different IDs during its lifetime if it is repeatedly moved between primary and secondary storage.

Systems such as Plessey and Intel solve this problem by using two formats for capabilities, an active form and a passive form (sometimes called an inform and outform). A simplified model of the use of active and passive capabilities follows. When each object is created, it is assigned an ID that is guaranteed to be unique for at least the life of the object (although not for all time). This ID might be generated by the physical disk address of the secondary storage for the object. All capabilities for the object, when stored on secondary memory, are kept in passive form. Passive capabilities contain this *long-term* ID.

When an object is brought into primary memory, it is allocated a mapping table descriptor. The mapping table index provides the *short-term* ID for that period of primary memory residency. When a capability is used as a reference, the hardware or software must be able to detect whether the capability is active or passive. An active capability will contain a short-term ID and can be used to directly access an object. A capability in passive form will cause a trap. The software can then examine the long-term ID in the passive capability and convert it to the short-term ID for the object in memory. Or, if the object is not currently in memory, it is swapped in and a descriptor and short-term ID are assigned.

When an object is removed from primary memory, its capabilities are converted to passive form for storage on disk. However, the system must ensure that no active capabilities exist for the object before its mapping table descriptor can be reallocated. Any remaining active capabilities must be in primary memory since they cannot be stored on disk. Therefore, the system can either maintain a reference count for active capabilities or search the C-lists of all resident processes to passivate any active capabilities for the object.

Another design decision to be made in managing secondary object storage is determining how and when an object's secondary storage copy will be updated. The operating system can manage virtual object storage, automatically moving objects between primary and secondary memory. This corresponds to swapping in conventional systems. However, this transparent storage mechanism does not ensure that an object's secondary memory copy is always up to date. Some applications need to guarantee that certain modifications will not be lost by a crash. Another scheme, then, is for the system to provide explicit checkpointing operations for type managers. A type manager performs temporary object modifications in memory and atomically outputs the object to permanent storage by requesting a checkpoint.

An additional problem with object storage is the use of transportable media. Object IDs may be unique for a single system, but are typically not unique for all systems. Moving an object from one computer system to another creates problems because the object's ID may be duplicated on the other system. Backup of objects provides a similar problem. Maintaining capability integrity on transportable media or over networks is an additional concern.

10.8 Object Locking

One advantage of capability systems is the ease with which objects can be shared among several users. This sharing poses problems when users of a shared object must perform multistep atomic transactions. That is, a user may need to execute several object operations with the assurance that no other user can access the same object until the transaction is complete. Exclusion is also required to prohibit a process from operating on inconsistent data when an I/O device is transmitting to object storage. Thus, locking facilities are provided in many capability systems.

The Intel 432 provides instructions to lock and unlock objects. A lock is simply a 16-bit field stored within the data part of a segment; the lock contains a 14-bit process ID and a 2-bit lock type. Objects can be locked either by hardware or software. Some system objects have locks in the processor—defined object data part. Hardware manipulates these locks to obtain exclusion when performing certain operations. Software uses the LOCK OBJECT and UNLOCK OBJECT instructions to obtain mutual exclusion to an object. Execution of a LOCK OBJECT instruction checks if the lock is free; if it is free, the process ID of the current process is stored in the lock and it is marked busy. The instruction returns a boolean result to indicate whether or not the instruction succeeded in obtaining the lock.

The IBM System/38 has a set of higher level lock operations to allow increased concurrency for database operations. Objects can be locked in one of five modes:

1. shared read—user can read, other users can read or write
2. shared read only—user can read, other users can read
3. shared update—user can read or write, other users can read or write
4. exclusive allow read—user can read or write, other users can only read
5. exclusive no read—user can read or write, other users cannot access

The LOCK OBJECT instruction requests one or more locks on one or more objects. The instruction will either succeed in obtaining all locks specified or no locks will be held; that is, if a lock cannot be obtained, all previous locks obtained by the instruction are released. The instruction can specify that the program either wait for locks that are currently unavailable or return immediately. There is also a time-out parameter that indicates the maximum time that the instruction should contend for a lock.

The horizontal microcode on the System/38 maintains a data structure that indicates (for each object for which a lock is held) the type of lock being held and the ID of the requester. Several locks may be held for a single object; this will be indicated in the data structure. The System/38 provides instructions to examine all locks held by a process or an object.

There are, thus, several basic types of locking facilities, including implicit and explicit locks. Implicit locks occur as the result of hardware manipulation of an object; this operation usually requires mutual exclusion. Software may request mutual exclusion or with more sophisticated mechanisms may request only certain types of exclusion to allow maximum concurrency.

10.9 Revocation

One strength of capability systems is the ability to copy and transmit object access rights freely between processes. This strength can also be a weakness when a user needs to restrict access to an object for which capabilities have previously been distributed. In this case, a *revocation* mechanism is needed to retract or cancel the outstanding capabilities. A good examination of such mechanisms is provided by Redell [Redell 74a]. With the exception of the System/38, none of the systems examined have attempted to support revocation.

The System/38 provides revocation through user profiles. Some System/38 capabilities (unauthorized capabilities) do not contain access rights. An object access that specifies such a capability requires a process-local profile table lookup to check the permitted access. The owner of an object can later revoke the object's access rights stored in another process's profile. This scheme combines the concept of access list with capability addressing. However, it adds some complexity to the use of capabilities because unauthorized capabilities require a profile search while authorized capabilities do not. Unauthorized capabilities are not context-independent and, therefore, cannot always be shared with other processes.

A program may wish to restrict capability access in other ways. For example, a calling procedure might want to ensure that a called program does not retain or pass on a capability parameter. The Hydra system provides access rights bits in the capability that specify whether a capability can be stored in a C-list with longer life than the procedure invocation.

Restriction of capability copying can be handled by access rights, but revocation is a more difficult problem. Only the System/38 has considered revocation an important facility to provide. Perhaps other systems have not been willing to pay the cost of the additional overhead. Or, more likely, they were not as concerned with the security and protection problems brought on by the easy propagation of capabilities. These problems will become more important to solve as capability systems find more acceptance in commercial applications.

10.10 Conclusions

This book has followed the history of capability systems from early descriptor machines and Iliffe's codewords, through the first designs by Dennis and Van Horn at MIT and Fabry at Chicago, to the most recent commercial systems by IBM and Intel. Capability systems are of great interest today because of the object approach that is affecting the design of languages, operating systems, and hardware. The object approach promises to influence to a large extent the way in which software is produced in the future.

There are a number of benefits to be gained from capability systems. Although many of these benefits have been described previously, some of the most important ones are restated here.

1. Capability systems permit great flexibility in dynamic sharing of information. This flexibility is due to the global, context-independent interpretation of capabilities, and the ability of users to copy and transmit capabilities freely. Sharing

of data structures does not require operating system intervention for mapping shared structures or for buffering information between processes.

2. Capabilities provide a single uniform mechanism for naming
objects of all types. Most traditional systems require many
different naming schemes for operating system objects as
well as hardware objects.

3. Capability systems provide a good basis for protection and
isolation of software components. A procedure's domain can
be restricted to include only those objects absolutely required for operation. Different procedures, even in the same
subsystem, can execute in disjoint, overlapping, or identical
domains. This protection mechanism aids in software reliability.

4. There is nothing "privileged" about protection on a capability system; that is, there is generally no privileged mode of
operation. The ability to access objects is defined by the
execution domain. Traditionally privileged software systems
can thus be implemented as standard user programs. Users
can add functions to the operating system base in a uniform
way without requiring special privilege.

5. Capability systems support a long-term, single-level object
storage system that removes the concept of secondary storage file systems.

6. Capability systems make an explicit distinction between
addresses and data. This distinction makes garbage collection of objects possible.

In addition to these advantages, there are a number of associated problems.

1. Capabilities and their associated mapping information can
consume additional storage space. For example, System/38
capabilities require 16 bytes of storage. Intel 432 capabilities
are only 32 bits in size, but the mapping tables require 16
bytes per object.

2. Garbage collection of the object space may be required to
locate objects that are no longer accessible. Garbage collection is a complex and resource consuming task.

3. Garbage collection of the name space may be required to
avoid dangling references whenever an object is destroyed.
The required capability search is particularly difficult on a
system that uses tagging of capabilities, because all memory
segments can potentially contain capabilities. On a system
using C-lists, only the capability segments need to be
searched, but this can still be a costly operation.

4. The advantages of protection and isolation are gained
through the use of a protected procedure mechanism. The
call or enter mechanism used to invoke a protected procedure can be expensive, since a new addressing environment

must be constructed. (A call on a capability system is analogous in many ways to a context switch on a conventional system.) This cost can force a programming style contrary to that intended. Although these mechanisms provide excellent support for small domains, they may prove expensive for subsystems that need to pass large, complex information structures.

5. Capability systems can be costly in the number of memory references needed to access an operand. Every operand reference requires access to a capability and to several mapping tables (although this overhead exists on any segmented or paged system). Systems with explicit capability registers seem better in this respect, and caches can help as well.

6. Whether or not capabilities can be used to build a secure system is still an open issue. Capability systems typically support unrestricted passing of information, while secure systems require controls on information passing. It is difficult in most capability systems (with the exception of System/38) to determine who has access to an object.

These lists indicate that capability mechanisms may increase programming generality and protection at the possible cost of performance. Although capability systems may simplify the construction of complex systems, they add new complexities to the hardware and operating system implementation. Still, the performance problems suffered by many early capability systems were often due to peculiarities of the individual designs or to hardware poorly matched to the task. There is probably no inherent reason why a capability-based system cannot perform as well as a conventional architecture machine.

It is the success or failure of the object-based programming approach that will eventually determine the success or failure of capability architectures. Although object-based programming can be supported by specialized languages on conventional machines, capability addressing provides run-time protection and error detection. Capabilities can support an environment with a mix of different object-based and conventional languages on the same machine. Whether or not the object approach allows programmers to handle the complexity inherent in sophisticated applications better remains to be demonstrated. We have surely seen only the first generation of object-based and capability-based systems to appear in the commercial marketplace.

Bibliography

[Ackerman 67]
  W. B. Ackerman and W. W. Plummer. An Implementation of a
  Multiprocessing Computer System. In *Proceedings of the ACM
  Symposium on Operating System Principles*. October 1967.

[Almes 78]
  G. Almes and G. Robertson. An Extensible File System for Hydra.
  In *Proceedings of 3rd International Conference on Software Engi-
  neering*, pages 288–294. ACM, May 1978.

[Almes 80]
  G. T. Almes. *Garbage Collection in an Object-Oriented System*.
  Ph.D. thesis, Carnegie-Mellon University, June 1980.

[Bell 76]
  G. Bell and W. D. Strecker. Computer Structures: What Have We
  Learned From the PDP-11? In *Proceedings of the 3rd Annual
  Symposium on Computer Architecture*, pages 1–14. January 1976.

[Bennett 82]
  J. K. Bennett. *A Comparison of Four Object-Oriented Systems*. Tech-
  nical Report TR 82-11-03, Department of Computer Science,
  University of Washington, 1982.

[Berstis 80a]
  V. Berstis. Security and Protection of Data in the IBM System/38.
  In *Proceedings of the 7th Symposium on Computer Architecture*,
  pages 245–252. May 1980.

[Berstis 80b]
  V. Berstis, C. D. Truxal and J. G. Ranweller. System/38 Addressing and Authorization. In *IBM System/38 Technical Developments*. IBM GSD G580-0237-1, 1980.

[Bierman 81]

E. M. Bierman. *A Comparative Study of Network-Based Object-Oriented File Systems*. Master's thesis, University of Washington, 1981.

[Birrell 78]

A. D. Birrell and R. M. Needham. An Asynchronous Garbage Collector for the CAP Filing Systems. *Operating Systems Review* 12(2):31–33, April 1978.

[Bishop 77]

P. B. Bishop. *Computer Systems with a Very Large Address Space and Garbage Collection*. Ph.D. thesis, MIT, May 1977.

[Brinch Hansen 78]

P. B. Hansen. Distributed Processes: A Concurrent Programming Concept. *Communications of the ACM* 24(11):934–941, November 1978.

[Burroughs 61]

The Descriptor—a Definition of the B5000 Information Processing System. Burroughs Corporation, Detroit, Michigan, 1961.

[Cohen 75]

E. Cohen and D. Jefferson. Protection in the Hydra Operating System. In *Proceedings of the 5th Symposium on Operating Systems Principles*, pages 141–160. November 1975.

[Cohen 76]

E. Cohen, W. Corwin, D. Jefferson, T. Lane, R. Levin, J. Newcomer, F. Pollack, and W. Wulf. *Hydra Kernel Reference Manual*. Department of Computer Science, Carnegie-Mellon University, 1976.

[Cook 78a]

D. Cook. The Cost of Using the CAP Computer's Protection Facilities. *Operating Systems Review* 12(1), April 1978.

[Cook 78b]

D. J. Cook. *The Evaluation of a Protection System*. Ph.D. thesis, University of Cambridge, 1978.

[Cook 79]

D. Cook. In Support of Domain Structure for Operating Systems. In *Proceedings of the 7th Symposium on Operating Systems Principles*, pages 128–130. December 1979.

[Cosserat 72]

D. C. Cosserat. A Capability Oriented Multi-Processor System for Real-Time Applications. In *Proceedings of the International Conference on Computer Communications*. October 1972.

[Cosserat 74]

D. C. Cosserat. A Data Model Based on the Capability Protection Mechanism. In *Proceedings of the International Workshop on Protection in Operating Systems*. August 1974.

[Cox 83]
G. W. Cox, W. M. Corwin, K. K. Lai, and F. J. Pollack. Inter-process Communication and Processor Dispatching on the Intel 432. *ACM Transactions on Computer Systems* 1(1), February 1983.

[Dahl 66]
O. J. Dahl and K. Nygaard. Simula—An Algol-Based Simulation Language. *Communications of the ACM* 9(9), September 1966.

[Dahlby 80]
S. H. Dahlby, G. G. Henry, D. N. Reynolds, and P. T. Taylor. System/38—a High-Level Machine. In *IBM System/38 Technical Developments*. IBM GSD G580-0237-1, 1980.

[Denning 76]
P. J. Denning. Fault-Tolerant Operating Systems. *Computing Surveys* 8(4), December 1976.

[Dennis 66]
J. B. Dennis and E. C. Van Horn. Programming Semantics for Multiprogrammed Computations. *Communications of the ACM* 9(3), March 1966.

[Dennis 80]
T. D. Dennis. *A Capability Architecture*. Ph.D. thesis, Purdue University, May 1980.

[Dijkstra 78]
E. W. Dijkstra, L. Lamport, A. M. Martin, C. S. Scholten, and E. F. M. Steffens. On-the-Fly Garbage Collection: An Exercise in Cooperation. *Communications of the ACM* 21(11), November 1978.

[DOD 80]
Reference Manual for the Ada Programming Language. United States Department of Defense, 1980.

[England 72a]
D. M. England. Architectural Features of System 250. In *Infotech State of the Art Report on Operating Systems*. Infotech, 1972.

[England 72b]
D. M. England. Operating System of System 250. In *Proceedings of International Switching Symposium*. June 1972.

[England 74]
D. M. England. Capability Concept Mechanism and Structure in System 250. In *Proceedings of the International Workshop on Protection in Operating Systems*. August 1974.

[Fabry 67]
R. Fabry. A User's View of Capabilities. In *ICR Quarterly Report*, pages C1–C8. U. of Chicago Institute for Computer Research, November 1967.

[Fabry 68]

R. S. Fabry. Preliminary Description of a Supervisor for a Machine Oriented Around Capabilities. In *ICR Quarterly Report*, pages B1–B97. U. of Chicago Institute for Computer Research, August 1968.

[Fabry 71]

R. S. Fabry. *List-Structured Addressing*. Ph.D. thesis, University of Chicago, March 1971.

[Fabry 74]

R. S. Fabry. Capability-Based Addressing. *Communications of the ACM* 17(7):403–412, July 1974.

[Feustel 72]

E. A. Feustel. The Rice Research Computer—A Tagged Architecture. In *Proceedings of the Spring Joint Computer Conference*, pages 369–377. IFIPS, 1972.

[Feustel 73]

E. A. Feustel. On the Advantages of Tagged Architectures. *IEEE Transactions on Computers* C-22(7):644–656, July 1973.

[Fuller 78]

S. H. Fuller and S. P. Harbison. *The C.mmp Multiprocessor*. Technical Report, Department of Computer Science, Carnegie-Mellon University, 1978.

[Gehringer 79]

E. F. Gehringer. Variable-Length Capabilities as a Solution to the Small-Object Problem. In *Proceedings of the 7th Symposium on Operating Systems Principles*, pages 131–142. December 1979.

[Gehringer 81]

E. F. Gehringer and R. J. Chansler, Jr. *STAROS User and System Structure Manual*, Department of Computer Science, Carnegie-Mellon University, 1981.

[Gehringer 82]

E. F. Gehringer. *Capability Architectures and Small Objects*. UMI Research Press, 1982.

[Goldberg 83]

A. Goldberg and D. Robson. *Smalltalk-80: The Language and Its Implementation*. Addison-Wesley, 1983.

[Goodenough 75]

J. B. Goodenough. Exception Handling: Issues and a Proposed Notation. *Communications of the ACM* 18(12):683–696, December 1975.

[Graham 72]

G. S. Graham and P. J. Denning. Protection—Principles and Practice. In *Proceedings of the Spring Joint Computer Conference*, pages 417–429. 1972.

[Halton 72]
D. Halton. Hardware of the System 250 for Communication Control. In *Proceedings of International Switching Symposium*. June 1972.

[Hamer-Hodges 72]
K. J. Hamer-Hodges. Fault Resistance and Recovery Within System 250. In *Proceedings of the International Conference on Computer Communications*. October 1972.

[Hamilton 79]
J. Hamilton. Location Dependencies in Distributed Operating Systems. In *Proceedings of the Louisiana Computer Exposition*. March 1979.

[Hansen 82]
P. M. Hansen, M. A. Linton, R. N. Mayo, M. Murphy, and D. A. Patterson. A Performance Evaluation of the Intel iAPX 432. *Computer Architecture News* 10(4):17–26, June 1982.

[Harrison 75]
M. A. Harrison, W. L. Ruzzo, and J. D. Ullman. On Protection in Operating Systems. In *Proceedings of the 5th Symposium on Operating Systems Principles*, pages 14–24. November 1975.

[Herbert 77a]
A. J. Herbert, editor. *CAP Hardware Manual*. Computer Laboratory, University of Cambridge, 1977.

[Herbert 77b]
A. J. Herbert, editor. *CAP System Programmer's Manual*. Computer Laboratory, University of Cambridge, 1977.

[Herbert 77c]
A. J. Herbert, editor. *CAP Operating System Manual*. Computer Laboratory, University of Cambridge, 1977.

[Herbert 78a]
A. J. Herbert. A New Protection Architecture for the Cambridge Capability Computer. *Operating Systems Review* 12(1), January 1978.

[Herbert 78b]
A. J. Herbert. *A Microprogrammed Operating System Kernel*. Ph.D. thesis, University of Cambridge, 1978.

[Herbert 79]
A. J. Herbert. A Hardware-Supported Protection Architecture. In D. Lanciaux, editor, *Operating Systems*. North Holland, 1979.

[Hoare 74]
C. A. R. Hoare. Monitors: An Operating System Structuring Concept. *Communications of the ACM* 17(10):549–557, October 1974.

[Hoch 80]
C. Hoch and J. C. Browne. An Implementation of Capabilities on the PDP-11/45. *Operating Systems Review* 14(3), July 1980.

[Hoffman 80]
R. L. Hoffman and F. G. Soltis. Hardware Organization of the System/38. In *IBM System/38 Technical Developments*. IBM GSD G580-0237-1, 1980.

[Houdek 80]
M. E. Houdek and G. R. Mitchell. Translating a Large Virtual Address. In *IBM System/38 Technical Developments*. IBM GSD G580-0237-1, 1980.

[Houdek 81]
M. E. Houdek, F. G. Soltis, and R. L. Hoffman. IBM System/38 Support for Capability-Based Addressing. In *Proceedings of the 8th Symposium on Computer Architecture*. ACM/IEEE, May 1981.

[HP 72]
HP 3000 Computer System Reference Manual. Hewlett-Packard Company, Cupertino, California, 1972.

[IBM 80]
IBM System/38 Functional Reference Manual. IBM GA21-9331-3, 1982.

[IBM 82a]
IBM System/38 Technical Developments. IBM GSD G580-0237-1, 1980. (A collection of 30 short papers on System/38).

[IBM 82b]
IBM System/38 Functional Concepts Manual. IBM GA21-9330-1, 1982.

[Iliffe 62]
J. K. Iliffe and J. G. Jodeit. A Dynamic Storage Allocation Scheme. *Computer Journal* 5(3):200–209, October 1962.

[Iliffe 68]
J. K. Iliffe. *Basic Machine Principles*. American Elsevier, Inc., New York, 1968.

[Iliffe 69]
J. K. Iliffe. Elements of BLM. *Computer Journal* 12(3):251–258, August 1969.

[Iliffe 82]
J. K. Iliffe. *Advanced Computer Design*. Prentice/Hall International, 1982.

[Ingalls 78]
D. H. H. Ingalls. The Smalltalk-76 Programming System Design and Implementation. In *Proceedings of the 5th ACM Symposium on Principles of Programming Languages*. January 1978.

[Ingalls 81]
D. H. H. Ingalls. Design Principles Behind Smalltalk. *Byte* 6(8), 1981.

[Intel 81]
iAPX 432 General Data Processor Architecture Reference Manual. Preliminary edition, Intel Corp., Aloha, Oregon, 1981.

[Intel 82]
iAPX 432 General Data Processor Architecture Reference Manual. Revision 3 (Advance Partial Issue) edition, Santa Clara, California, 1982.

[Jagannathan 80]
A. Jagannathan. A Technique for the Architectural Implementation of Software Subsystems. In *Proceedings of the 7th Symposium on Computer Architecture*, pages 236–244. May 1980.

[Jensen 75]
K. Jensen and N. Wirth. *Pascal User Manual and Report.* Springer-Verlag, 1975.

[Jodeit 68]
J. G. Jodeit. Storage Organization in Programming Systems. *Communications of the ACM* 11(11), November 1968.

[Jones 73]
A. K. Jones. *Protection in Programmed Systems.* Ph.D. thesis, Carnegie-Mellon University, June 1973.

[Jones 78a]
A. K. Jones, R. J. Chansler, Jr., I. Durham, K. Schwans and S. R. Vegdahl. STAROS, A Multiprocessor Operating System for the Support of Task Forces. In *Proceeding of the 7th Symposium on Operating Systems Principles*, pages 117–127. December 1978.

[Jones 78b]
A. K. Jones. The Object Model: A Conceptual Tool for Structuring Software. In R. Bayer, R.M. Graham, and G. Seegmuller, (editors), *Operating Systems—An Advanced Course.* Springer-Verlag, 1978.

[Jones 80a]
A. K. Jones and E. F. Gehringer, editors. *The Cm* Multiprocessor Project: A Research Review.* Technical Report, Department of Computer Science, Carnegie-Mellon University, July 1980.

[Jones 80b]
A. K. Jones. Capability Architecture Revisited. *Operating Systems Review* 14(3), July 1980.

[Kaehler 81]
T. Kaehler. Virtual Memory for an Object-Oriented Language. *Byte* 6(8), August 1981.

213

[Kahn 81]

K. C. Kahn, W. M. Corwin, T. D. Dennis, H. D'Hooge, D. E. Hubka, L. A. Hutchins, J. T. Montague, and F. J. Pollack. iMAX: A Multiprocessor Operating System for an Object-Based Computer. In *Proceedings of the 8th Symposium on Operating System Principles*. December 1981.

[Krasner 81]

G. Krasner. The Smalltalk-80 Virtual Machine. *Byte* 6(8), 1981.

[Lampson 69]

B. W. Lampson. Dynamic Protection Structures. In *Proceedings of Fall Joint Computer Conference*, pages 27–38. IFIPS, 1969.

[Lampson 71]

B. W. Lampson. Protection. In *Proceedings of the Fifth Princeton Symposium on Information Sciences and Systems*, pages 437–443. March 1971. Reprinted in *Operating Systems Review*, 8(1), January 1974.

[Lampson 76]

B. W. Lampson and H. E. Sturgis. Reflections on an Operating System Design. *Communications of the ACM* 19(5):251–265, May 1976.

[Lampson 80]

B. W. Lampson and D. P. Redell. Experience with Processes and Monitors in Mesa. *Communications of the ACM* 23(2):105–117, February 1980.

[Lazowska 81]

E. D. Lazowska, H. M. Levy, G. T. Almes, M. J. Fischer, R. J. Fowler, and S. C. Vestal. The Architecture of the Eden System. In *Proceedings of the 8th Symposium on Operating Systems Principles*. December 1981.

[Levin 75]

R. Levin, E. Cohen, W. Corwin, F. Pollack, and W. Wulf. Policy/ Mechanism Separation in Hydra. In *Proceedings of the 5th Symposium on Operating Systems Principles*, pages 132–140. November 1975.

[Levin 77]

R. Levin. *Program Structures for Exceptional Condition Handling.* Ph.D. thesis, Carnegie-Mellon University, June 1977.

[Levy 81]

H. M. Levy. *A Comparative Study of Capability-Based Computer Architectures.* Master's thesis, University of Washington, 1981.

[Linden 76]

T. A. Linden. Operating System Structures to Support Security and Reliable Software. *Computing Surveys* 8(4), December 1976.

[Liskov 77]

B. Liskov, A. Snyder, R. Atkinson, and C. Schaffert. Abstraction

Mechanisms in CLU. *Communications of the ACM*
20(8):564–576, August 1977.

[Liskov 79a]
B. H. Liskov and A. Snyder. Exception Handling in CLU. *IEEE Transactions on Software Engineering* (6):546–558, October 1979.

[Liskov 79b]
B. Liskov, R. Atkinson, T. Bloom, E. Moss, C. Schaffert, B. Scheifler, and A. Snyder. *CLU Reference Manual.* Technical Report LCS/TR-225, MIT, October 1979.

[Luniewski 79]
A. W. Luniewski. *The Architecture of an Object Based Personal Computer.* Ph.D. thesis, MIT, 1979.

[MIT 71]
PDP-1 Computer Instruction Manual, Part 5—MTA's and IVK's. Electrical Engineering Department Document PDP-35-1, MIT, Cambridge, Mass., 1971.

[Morris 73a]
J. H. Morris, Jr., Types Are Not Sets. In *Symposium on the Principles of Programming Languages,* pages 120–121. October 1973.

[Morris 73b]
J. H. Morris, Jr. Protection in Programming Languages. *Communications of the ACM* 16(1):15–21, January 1973.

[Myers 80]
G. J. Myers and B. R. S. Buckingham. A Hardware Implementation of Capability-Based Addressing. *Operating Systems Review* 14(4), October 1980.

[Myers 82]
G. J. Myers. *Advances in Computer Architecture,* Second Edition. John Wiley & Sons, 1982.

[Needham 72]
R. M. Needham. Protection Systems and Protection Implementations. In *Proceedings of the Fall Joint Computer Conference,* pages 571–578. 1972.

[Needham 74]
R. M. Needham and M. V. Wilkes. Domains of Protection and the Management of Processes. *The Computer Journal* 17(2), 1974.

[Needham 77a]
R. M. Needham and R. D. H. Walker. The Cambridge CAP Computer and its Protection System. In *Proceedings of the 6th Symposium on Operating System Principles,* pages 1–10. November 1977.

[Needham 77b]
R. M. Needham. The CAP Project—an Interim Evaluation. In *Proceedings of the 6th Symposium on Operating System Principles,* pages 17–22. November 1977.

[Needham 77c]
R. M. Needham and A. D. Birrell. The CAP Filing System. In *Proceedings of the 6th Symposium on Operating System Principles*, pages 11–16. November 1977.

[Organick 83]
E. I. Organick. *A Programmer's View of the Intel 432 System*. McGraw-Hill, 1983.

[Ousterhout 80a]
J. K. Ousterhout, D. A. Scelza, and P. S. Sindhu. Medusa: An Experiment in Distributed Operating System Structure. *Communications of the ACM* 23(2), February 1980.

[Ousterhout 80b]
J. K. Ousterhout. *Partitioning and Cooperation in a Distributed Multiprocessor Operating System: Medusa*. Ph.D. thesis, Carnegie-Mellon University, April 1980.

[Parnas 72]
D. L. Parnas. On The Criteria To Be Used In Decomposing Systems Into Modules. *Communications of the ACM* 15(12), December 1972.

[Pashtan 82]
A. Pashtan. Object Oriented Operating Systems: An Emerging Design Methodology. In *Proceedings of ACM 82*, pages 126–131. October 1982.

[Pinnow 80]
K. W. Pinnow, J. G. Ranweller, and J. F. Miller. System/38 Object-Oriented Architecture. In *IBM System/38 Technical Developments*. IBM GSD G580-0237-1, 1980.

[Pollack 81]
F. J. Pollack, K. C. Kahn, and R. M. Wilkinson. The iMAX-432 Object Filing System. In *Proceedings of the 8th Symposium on Operating System Principles*. December 1981.

[Pollack 82]
F. J. Pollack, G. W. Cox, D. W. Hammerstrom, K. C. Kahn, K. K. Lai, and J. R. Rattner. Supporting Ada Memory Management in the iAPX-432. In *Proceedings of the Symposium on Architectural Support for Programming Languages and Operating Systems*, pages 117–131. March 1982.

[Rattner 81]
J. Rattner and W. W. Lattin. Ada Determines Architecture of 32-bit Microprocessor. *Electronics* 54(4), February 24, 1981.

[Redell 74a]
D. D. Redell. *Naming and Protection in Extendible Operating Systems*. Ph.D. thesis, University of California, Berkeley, September 1974. Available also as MIT project MAC TR-140.

[Redell 74b]
   D. Redell and R. Fabry. Selective Revocation of Capabilities. In *International Workshop on Protection in Operating Systems*. IRIA, August 1974.

[Saltzer 74]
   J. H. Saltzer. Protection and the Control of Information Sharing in Multics. *Communications of the ACM* 17(7):388–402, July 1974.

[Saltzer 75]
   J. H. Saltzer and M. D. Schroeder. The Protection of Information in Computer Systems. *Proceedings of the IEEE* 63(9), September 1975.

[Shepherd 68]
   J. H. Shepherd. Principal Design Features of the Multi-Computer. In *ICR Quarterly Report*, pages C1–C13. U. of Chicago Institute for Computer Research, November 1968.

[Snyder 79]
   A. Snyder. *A Machine Architecture to Support an Object-Oriented Language*. Ph.D. thesis, MIT, March 1979.

[Soltis 79]
   F. G. Soltis and R. L. Hoffman. Design Considerations for the IBM System/38. In *Proceedings of Compcon 79*. Spring 1979.

[Soltis 81]
   F. G. Soltis. Design of a Small Business Data Processing System. *Computer*, September 1981.

[Spier 73]
   M. J. Spier, T. N. Hastings, and D. N. Cutler. An Experimental Implementation of the Kernel/Domain Architecture. In *Proceedings of the Fourth Symposium on Operating System Principles*, pages 8–21. October 1973.

[Sturgis 74]
   H. E. Sturgis. *A Postmortem for a Timesharing System*. Ph.D. thesis, University of California, Berkeley, 1974. Reprinted as Xerox Parc report CSL-74-1.

[Swan 78]
   R. J. Swan. *The Switching Structure and Addressing Architecture of an Extensible Multiprocessor: Cm**. Ph.D. thesis, Carnegie-Mellon University, August 1978.

[Walker 73]
   R. D. H. Walker. *The Structure of a Well-Protected Computer*. Ph.D. thesis, University of Cambridge, 1973.

[Wilkes 68]
   M. V. Wilkes. *Time-Sharing Computer Systems*. American Elsevier, Inc., New York, 1968.

[Wilkes 79]

M. V. Wilkes and R. M. Needham. *The Cambridge CAP Computer and its Operating System.* North Holland, New York, 1979.

[Wilkes 82]

M. V. Wilkes. Hardware Support for Memory Protection. In *Proceedings of the Symposium on Architectural Support for Programming Languages and Operating Systems,* pages 107–116. March 1982.

[Wulf 74a]

W. Wulf, E. Cohen, W. Corwin, A. Jones, R. Levin, C. Pierson, and F. Pollack. Hydra: The Kernel of a Multiprocessor Operating System. *Communications of the ACM* 17(6), June 1974.

[Wulf 74b]

W. A. Wulf. *Alphard: Toward a Language to Support Structured Programs.* Technical Report, Carnegie-Mellon University, Computer Science Department, 1974.

[Wulf 75]

W. Wulf, R. Levin, and C. Pierson. Overview of the Hydra Operating System Development. In *Proceedings of the Fifth Symposium on Operating Systems Principles,* pages 122–131. November 1975.

[Wulf 78]

W. A. Wulf, and S. P. Harbison. Reflections in a Pool of Processors: An Experience Report on C.mmp. In *1978 National Computer Conference.* AFIPS Press, 1978.

[Wulf 81]

W. A. Wulf, R. Levin, and S. P. Harbison. *HYDRA/C.mmp: An Experimental Computer System.* McGraw-Hill, New York, 1981.

[Yngve 68]

V. H. Yngve. The Chicago Magic Number Computer. In *ICR Quarterly Report,* pages B1–B20. U. of Chicago Institute for Computer Research, November 1968.

[Zeigler 81]

S. Zeigler, N. Allegre, R. Johnson, and J. Morris. Ada for the Intel 432 Microcomputer. *Computer* 14(6):47–56, June 1981.

Index

Access control list, 148
Addressing
  on Basic Language Machine, 33
  on CAL-TSS, 54
  on CAP, 81, 84, 86
  on Chicago Magic Number
    Machine, 50
  on Hydra, 120
  on Intel 432, 163
  on Plessey 250, 71
  on StarOS, 131
  on System/38, 141, 145

Basic Language Machine, 30
Burroughs B5000, 22

C.mmp, 103–105, 127
CAL-TSS system, 52
Cambridge CAP computer, 79
CAP capability unit, 89
Capabilities, 187, 191
  on CAL-TSS, 53
  on CAP, 83, 92
  on Chicago Magic Number
    Machine, 49
  on Dennis and Van Horn
    Supervisor, 42
  on Hydra, 111, 120
  on Intel 432, 165
  on MIT PDP-1 System, 47

  on Plessey 250, 67
  on StarOS, 130
  on System/38, 142
Capability operations
  on Chicago Magic Number
    Machine, 50
  on Dennis and Van Horn
    Supervisor, 43
  on Hydra, 110
  on Intel 432, 166
  on System/38, 144
CDC 6400, 52
Chicago Magic Number Machine, 48
CM*, 127
CPF, 137
Codewords
  on Basic Language Machine, 31
  on Rice University Computer, 26
  See also Descriptors

Data tagging
  on Basic Language Machine, 32
Dennis and Van Horn, 41
Descriptors
  on B5000, 23
  See also Codewords
Directories, 44, 132
Domain, 42
  on CAL-TSS, 53

Garbage collection, 121, 131, 197
Global Symbol Table, 118

Hydra System, 103

Intel 8086, 160
Intel iAPX 432, 159

Local name space, 109
LSI-11, 127

Medusa, 128
MIT PDP-1 timesharing system, 47
Multiprogramming, 21

Object locking, 201
Object Table Directory, 164
Objects, 195
    on Hydra, 105
    on Intel 432, 162
    on StarOS, 129
    on System/38, 139
Operations, *See* Capability operations

PDP-1, 47
PDP-11, 104, 109, 192
Plessey System 250, 65
Pointer resolution, 148
Process resource list, 85
Profile adoption, 153
Program Reference Table, 23

Protected procedures, 196
    on CAP, 90
    on Chicago Magic Number
        Machine, 51
    on Dennis and Van Horn
        Supervisor, 45
    on Hydra, 113
    on Intel 432, 173
    on MIT PDP-1 System, 48
    on Plessey 250, 72
    on System/38, 153

Reference counts, 121
Revocation, 148, 202
Rice University Computer, 25

Segmentation, 21, 188
Sphere of protection, 42
StarOS, 127, 128
System/38, 137

Tag, 32
Task forces, 128
Type extension, 196
    on CAL-TSS, 55
    on CAP, 94
    on Hydra, 113
    on Intel 432, 176
    on MIT PDP-1 System, 48
    on Plessey 250, 73
    on StarOS, 133
TYPECALL, 116